Q: Skills for Success

READING AND WRITING

INTRO

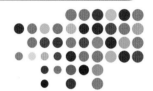

Jennifer Bixby

Joe McVeigh

SERIES CONSULTANTS

Marguerite Ann Snow

Lawrence J. Zwier

VOCABULARY CONSULTANT

Cheryl Boyd Zimmerman

OXFORD

UNIVERSITY PRESS

OXFORD
UNIVERSITY PRESS

198 Madison Avenue
New York, NY 10016 USA

Great Clarendon Street, Oxford, OX2 6DP, United Kingdom

Oxford University Press is a department of the University of Oxford.
It furthers the University's objective of excellence in research, scholarship,
and education by publishing worldwide. Oxford is a registered trade
mark of Oxford University Press in the UK and in certain other countries.

General Manager, American ELT: Laura Pearson

Publisher: Stephanie Karras

Associate Publishing Manager: Sharon Sargent

Senior Development Editor: Andrew Gitzy

Associate Development Editors: Rebecca Mostov, Keyana Shaw

Director, ADP: Susan Sanguily

Executive Design Manager: Maj-Britt Hagsted

Associate Design Manager: Michael Steinhofer

Electronic Production Manager: Julie Armstrong

Production Artist: Elissa Santos

Cover Design: Molly Scanlon

Image Manager: Trisha Masterson

Image Editor: Liaht Pashayan

Production Coordinator: Elizabeth Matsumoto

ISBN: 978 0 19 475650 1 READING AND WRITING INTRO
STUDENT BOOK PACK

ISBN: 978 0 19 475648 8 READING AND WRITING INTRO
STUDENT BOOK

ISBN: 978 0 19 475621 1 Q ONLINE PRACTICE
STUDENT ACCESS CODE CARD

Printed in China

This book is printed on paper from certified and well-managed sources.

ACKNOWLEDGEMENTS

The publishers would like to thank the following for their kind permission to reproduce photographs:
Cover Yukmin/Asia Images/Getty Images; Jupiter Images/Workbook Stock/Getty Images;
David Anderson/istockphoto; 4x6/istockphoto; Kuzma/istockphoto; TrapdoorMedia/
istockphoto; vi Marcin Krygier/istockphoto; xiii Rüstem Gürler/istockphoto; p. 2
Michael Steinhofer; p. 4 John Giustina/Getty Images (outgoing); p. 4 Eyecandy Images/
Alamy (fashionable); p. 4 Radius Images/Corbis (messy); p. 5 Jose Luis Pelaez, Inc./Blend
Images/Corbis; p. 6 Jupiterimages/Getty Images (basketball); p. 6 PhotosIndia.com/Getty
Images (reading); p. 8 Felix Mizioznikov/shutterstock.com (hat); p. 8 Tom Stewart/Corbis
(computer); p. 10 Angel Martinez/Real Madrid via Getty Images; p. 13 Allana Wesley
White/Corbis; p. 14 amana images inc./Alamy; p. 16 Plush Studios/Getty Images; p. 18
NetPhotos/Alamy; p. 25 Ocean/Corbis; p. 26 Scott Stulberg/SuperStock; p. 28 Sunny_baby/
shutterstock.com (texting); p. 28 Shannon Fagan/Blend Images/Corbis (man smiling);
p. 30 Rob Lewine/Tetra Images/Corbis; p. 34 PNC/Getty Images; p. 36 Darren Greenwood/
Design Pics/Corbis; p. 37 David Young-Wolff/Getty Images (Hispanic girl); p. 37 Danita
Delimont/Alamy (Kenyan boy); p. 38 ColorBlind Images/Getty Images; p. 40 Ariel Skelley/
Corbis; p. 41 Kristian Buus/In Pictures/Corbis; p. 43 Simon Jarratt/Corbis; p. 48 Sollina
Images/Getty Images; p. 50 Laurie Rubin/Masterfile (tomatoes); p. 50 JLP/Jose L. Pelaez/
Corbis (New Years Eve); p. 50 Dewitt/shutterstock.com (watermelon); p. 50 Stock
Connection Blue/Alamy (turkey); p. 51 KHAM/X01568/Reuters/Corbis (Tet preparations);
p. 51 Argus Photo/Alamy (rice cakes); p. 52 Sarah Bossert/istockphoto.com (black-eyed
peas); p. 52 World Religions Photo Library/Alamy (Norwuz); p. 57 Monkey Business Images/
shutterstock.com; p. 60 Sollina Images/Getty Images; p. 62 Mark Segal/age fotostock;
p. 65 Cavan Images/Getty Images; p. 66 D. Hurst/Alamy (Anna); p. 66 Toronto Star/age
fotostock (basketball); p. 66 Gawrav Sinha/Getty Images (Razi); p. 66 Andreas Stamm/
fstop/Corbis (kitchen); p. 66 David Young-Wolff/Getty Images (Sun-Hee); p. 66 Juice Images/
Alamy (Carlos); p. 66 Rick Gomez/age fotostock (Isabel); p. 67 Asia Images Group/Getty
Images (Khalid); p. 67 Ian Coble/Getty Images (Rob); p. 67 David Ashley/Corbis (London);
p. 67 Cavan Images/Getty Images (James); p. 68 Zhuoming Liang/Corbis (video camera);
p. 68 Siri Stafford/Getty Images (driving); p. 69 Rick Gomez/Masterfile;
p. 70 picturesbyrob/Alamy (highlighter); p. 70 Quique Kierszenbaum/Getty Images (story
telling); p. 71 Tim Kitchen/Getty Images; p. 76 David Askham/Alamy; p. 79 Nir Alon/Alamy;
p. 80 Corbis RF/Alamy (fireplace); p. 80 Juice Images/Alamy (teen with skateboard);
p. 80 MBI/Alamy (family dinner); p. 80 Clynt Garnham Germany/Alamy (foosball);
p. 84 Benjamin Benschneider/The Seattle Times; p. 90 Patti McConville/Getty Images
(living room); p. 90 Neo Vision/Getty Images (home office); p. 91 Douglas Keister/
Corbis (garage); p. 91 Kinn Deacon/Alamy (classroom); p. 94 Roy Langstaff/Alamy;
p. 96 Oswald Eckstein/Corbis; p. 97 Alan Copson/Getty Images (London); p. 97 Mike Theiss/
Ultimate Chase/Corbis (Mt. Washington); p. 98 Clive Rose/Getty Images (rain);
p. 98 Jean-Claude Winkler/Getty Images (desert); p. 98 John Goodge/National Science
Foundation (Antarctica); p. 101 Photostock-Israel/Science Photo Library (cockpit);
p. 101 Jim Reed/CORBIS (lightning); p. 102 Melanie Metz/shutterstock.com (tornado);
p. 102 Jim Edds/Science Photo Library (hurricane); p. 102 Digital Vision/Oxford University
Press (lightning); p. 103 AP Photo/Andres Leighton (beach during hurricane); p. 103 AP
Photo/Dave Martin (storm chaser); p. 103 Carsten Peter/National Geographic Stock (storm
chaser); p. 104 Ryan McGinnis/Alamy; p. 105 Ellen McKnight/Oxford University Press
(snow storm); p. 105 photo 24/Getty Images (sand storm); p. 112 John Rensten/age
fotostock; p. 114 Marco Andras/age fotostock; p. 117 Judith Collins/Oxford University
Press; p. 118 3d4Medical/Corbis; p. 120 Ocean/Corbis (video game); p. 120 Trae
Patton/NBCU Photo Bank via AP Images (The Biggest Loser); p. 123 Orange Line Media/
shutterstock.com; p. 125 age fotostock/SuperStock; p. 126 Dana Hursey/Masterfile;
p. 127 Max Paris/Alamy; p. 130 Andrew F. Kazmierski/shutterstock.com; p. 132 Glow
Asia RF/Alamy; p. 133 WoodyStock/Alamy; p. 134 David Grossman/Alamy (New York
City); p. 134 Atlantide Phototravel/Corbis (Spain); p. 134 Hisham Ibrahim/Getty Images
(Vancouver); p. 136 age fotostock/SuperStock (friends on street); p. 136 Lonely Planet/
SuperStock (playground); p. 136 Andy Hockridge/Alamy (park bench); p. 137 John Harper/
Corbis; p. 139 imagebroker.net/SuperStock (Humboldt University); p. 139 Sean Gallup/
Getty Images (Berlin market); p. 140 Grant Farquhar/Alamy; p. 141 Shawn Hempel/
shutterstock.com; p. 142 Richard Cummins/SuperStock; p. 144 Danita Delimont/Getty
Images; p. 145 Fraser Hall/Getty Images; p. 148 Brooks Kraft/Corbis; p. 151 age fotostock/
SuperStock; p. 152 Courtesy of Room to Read; p. 153 Ryan Smith/Somos Images/Corbis;
p. 155 Kelley L Cox/ZUMA Press/Corbis; p. 156 Getty Images; p. 157 Jeffrey Ufberg/Getty
Images for Barnes & Noble (Wood); p. 157 Kelley L Cox/ZUMA Press/Corbis (VanDerveer);
p. 159 Jim West/Alamy; p. 161 Gene Chutka/istockphoto.com; p. 163 Fotokia/Getty Images.

Illustrations by: p. 4 Stuart Bradford; p. 11 Stacy Merlin; p. 16 Stacy Merlin; p. 22 Greg
Paprocki; p. 32 Stacy Merlin; p. 65 Stuart Bradford; p. 88 Greg Paprocki; p. 92 Karen Minot;
p. 108 Stuart Bradford; p. 116 Karen Minot.

ACKNOWLEDGEMENTS

Authors

Jennifer Bixby received a B.A. in Comparative Literature from Washington University in St. Louis and holds an M.A. in TESOL from Boston University. She has taught students of various ages in Colombia, Japan, and Boston in a wide variety of programs, including community colleges and intensive English programs in the U.S. Her interests lie in the development of high-interest materials and in the teaching of writing. She is a frequent presenter at TESOL on topics related to materials development and reading skills.

Joe McVeigh holds a B.A. in English and American Literature from Brown University and an M.A. in TESOL from Biola University. He has taught at Middlebury College, the University of Southern California, the California Institute of Technology, and California State University, Los Angeles. Joe has also lived and worked overseas in the U.K., Hungary, China, India, and Chile. He has presented nationally and internationally on topics including methods and techniques for teaching reading, intercultural communication, and testing and assessment. He works independently as a consultant, teacher-trainer, workshop presenter, author, and editor.

Series Consultants

Marguerite Ann Snow holds a Ph.D. in Applied Linguistics from UCLA. She is a Professor in the Charter College of Education at California State University, Los Angeles where she teaches in the TESOL M.A. program. She has published in *TESOL Quarterly*, *Applied Linguistics*, and *The Modern Language Journal*. She has been a Fulbright scholar in Hong Kong and Cyprus. In 2006, she received the President's Distinguished Professor award at Cal State LA. In addition to working closely with ESL and mainstream public school teachers in the U.S., she has trained EFL teachers in Algeria, Argentina, Brazil, Egypt, Japan, Morocco, Pakistan, Spain, and Turkey. Her main interests are integrated content and language instruction, English for Academic Purposes, and standards for English teaching and learning.

Lawrence J. Zwier holds an M.A. in TESL from the University of Minnesota. He is currently the Associate Director for Curriculum Development at the English Language Center at Michigan State University in East Lansing. He has taught ESL/EFL in the U.S., Saudi Arabia, Malaysia, Japan, and Singapore. He is a frequent TESOL conference presenter and has published many ESL/EFL books in the areas of test-preparation, vocabulary, and reading, including *Inside Reading 2* for Oxford University Press.

Vocabulary Consultant

Cheryl Boyd Zimmerman is Associate Professor of TESOL at California State University, Fullerton. She specializes in second-language vocabulary acquisition, an area in which she is widely published. She teaches graduate courses on second-language acquisition, culture, vocabulary, and the fundamentals of TESOL and is a frequent invited speaker on topics related to vocabulary teaching and learning. She is the author of *Word Knowledge: A Vocabulary Teacher's Handbook* and Series Director of *Inside Reading*, both published by Oxford University Press.

Special thanks to our Introductory level advisors:

Aftab Ahmed, American University of Sharjah, U.A.E.; **Grace Bishop**, Houston Community College, TX; **Dr. İlke Büyükduman**, Istanbul Şehir University, Turkey; **Julie Carey**, American Language Institute, CA; **Pauline Koyess Chahine**, Qatar Armed Forces Language School, Qatar; **Yuwen Catherine Chen**, Eden English, Taichung; **Marta O. Dmytrenko-Ahrabian**, Wayne State University, MI; **Angela Donovan**, Language Studies International, NY; **Joan Fiser**, Sequoia High School, CA; **Kathleen Golata**, Galileo Academy, CA; **Janet Harclerode**, Santa Monica College, CA; **Hassan Hawash**, Abu Dhabi Men's College, U.A.E.; **Hui-min Hung**, Hot English School, Kaohsiung; **Mark Landa**, Mukogawa Women's University, Japan; **Renee LaRue**, Lone Star College–Montgomery, TX; **Janet Langon**, Glendale Community College, CA; **Paula Lee**, West Valley-Mission Community College District, CA; **Amy Ma**, Hot English School, Kaohsiung; **Neil McBeath**, Sultan Qaboos University, Oman; **Myles Grogan**, Momoyama Gakuin Daigaku, Japan; **Ahmed Ra'ef**, Saudi Academy, Saudi Arabia; **Leslie Ramirez**, Pasadena Memorial High School, TX; **Richard Seltzer**, Glendale Community College, CA; **Yusuf Şen**, Düzce University, Turkey; **Christine Tierney**, Houston Community College, TX; **Nathan Vasarhely**, Ygnacio Valley High School, CA; **Robert Wenn**, Abu Dhabi Men's College, U.A.E.

REVIEWERS

We would like to acknowledge the advice of teachers from all over the world who participated in online reviews, focus groups, and editorial reviews. We relied heavily on teacher input throughout the extensive development process of the Q series, and many of the features in the series came directly from feedback we gathered from teachers in the classroom. We are grateful to all who helped.

UNITED STATES **Marcarena Aguilar**, North Harris College, TX; **Deborah Anholt**, Lewis and Clark College, OR; **Robert Anzelde**, Oakton Community College, IL; **Arlys Arnold**, University of Minnesota, MN; **Marcia Arthur**, Renton Technical College, WA; **Anne Bachmann**, Clackamas Community College, OR; **Ron Balsamo**, Santa Rosa Junior College, CA; **Lori Barkley**, Portland State University, OR; **Eileen Barlow**, SUNY Albany, NY; **Sue Bartch**, Cuyahoga Community College, OH; **Lora Bates**, Oakton High School, VA; **Nancy Baum**, University of Texas at Arlington, TX; **Linda Berendsen**, Oakton Community College, IL; **Jennifer Binckes Lee**, Howard Community College, MD; **Grace Bishop**, Houston Community College, TX; **Jean W. Bodman**, Union County College, NJ; **Virginia Bouchard**, George Mason University, VA; **Kimberley Briesch Sumner**, University of Southern California, CA; **Gabriela Cambiasso**, Harold Washington College, IL; **Jackie Campbell**, Capistrano Unified School District, CA; **Adele C. Camus**, George Mason University, VA; **Laura Chason**, Savannah College, GA; **Kerry Linder Catana**, Language Studies International, NY; **An Cheng**, Oklahoma State University, OK; **Carole Collins**, North Hampton Community College, PA; **Betty R. Compton**, Intercultural Communications College, HI; **Pamela Couch**, Boston University, MA; **Fernanda Crowe**, Intrax International Institute, CA; **Margo Czinski**, Washtenaw Community College, MI; **David Dahnke**, Lone Star College, TX; **Gillian M. Dale**, CA; **L. Dalgish**, Concordia College, MN; **Christopher Davis**, John Jay College, NY; **Sonia Delgadillo**, Sierra College, CA; **Marta O. Dmytrenko-Ahrabian**, Wayne State University, MI; **Javier Dominguez**, Central High School, SC; **Jo Ellen Downey-Greer**, Lansing Community College, MI; **Jennifer Duclos**, Boston University, MA; **Yvonne Duncan**, City College of San Francisco, CA; **Jennie Farnell**, University of Connecticut, CT; **Susan Fedors**, Howard Community College, MD; **Matthew Florence**, Intrax International Institute, CA; **Kathleen Flynn**, Glendale College, CA; **Eve Fonseca**, St. Louis Community College, MO; **Elizabeth Foss**, Washtenaw Community College, MI; **Duff C. Galda**, Pima Community College, AZ; **Christiane Galvani**, Houston Community College, TX; **Gretchen Gerber**, Howard Community College, MD; **Ray Gonzalez**, Montgomery College, MD; **Alyona Gorokhova**, Grossmont College, CA; **John Graney**, Santa Fe College, FL; **Kathleen Green**, Central High School, AZ; **Webb Hamilton**, De Anza College, San Jose City College, CA; **Janet Harclerode**, Santa Monica Community College, CA; **Sandra Hartmann**, Language and Culture Center, TX; **Kathy Haven**, Mission College, CA; **Adam Henricksen**, University of Maryland, MD; **Peter Hoffman**, LaGuardia Community College, NY; **Linda Holden**, College of Lake County, IL; **Jana Holt**, Lake Washington Technical College, WA; **Gail Ibele**, University of Wisconsin, WI; **Mandy Kama**, Georgetown University, Washington, DC; **Stephanie Kasuboski**, Cuyahoga Community College, OH; **Chigusa Katoku**, Mission College, CA; **Sandra Kawamura**, Sacramento City College, CA; **Gail Kellersberger**, University of Houston–Downtown, TX; **Jane Kelly**, Durham Technical Community College, NC; **Julie Park Kim**, George Mason University, VA; **Lisa Kovacs-Morgan** University of California, San Diego, CA; **Claudia Kupiec**, DePaul University, IL; **Renee La Rue**, Lone Star College-Montgomery, TX; **Janet Langon**, Glendale College, CA; **Lawrence Lawson**, Palomar College, CA; **Rachele Lawton**, The Community College of Baltimore County, MD; **Alice Lee**, Richland College, TX; **Cherie Lenz-Hackett**, University of Washington, WA; **Joy Leventhal**, Cuyahoga Community College, OH; **Candace Lynch-Thompson**, North Orange County Community College District, CA; **Thi Thi Ma**, City College of San Francisco, CA; **Denise Maduli-Williams**, City College of San Francisco, CA; **Eileen Mahoney**, Camelback High School, AZ; **Brigitte Maronde**, Harold Washington College, IL; **Keith Maurice**, University of Texas at Arlington, TX; **Nancy Mayer**, University of Missouri-St. Louis, MO; **Karen Merritt**, Glendale Union High School District, AZ; **Holly Milkowart**, Johnson County Community College, KS; **Eric Moyer**, Intrax International Institute, CA; **Gino Muzzatti**, Santa Rosa Junior College, CA; **William Nedrow**, Triton College, IL; **Eric Nelson**, University of Minnesota, MN; **Rhony Ory**, Ygnacio Valley High School, CA; **Paul Parent**, Montgomery College, MD; **Oscar Pedroso**, Miami Dade College, FL; **Robin Persiani**, Sierra College, CA; **Patricia Prenz-Belkin**, Hostos Community College, NY; **Jim Ranalli**, Iowa State University, IA; **Toni R. Randall**, Santa Monica College, CA; **Vidya Rangachari**, Mission College, CA; **Elizabeth Rasmussen**, Northern Virginia Community College, VA; **Lara Ravitch**, Truman College, IL; **Deborah Repasz**, San Jacinto College, TX; **Andrey Reznikov**, Black Hills State University, SD; **Alison Rice**, Hunter College, NY; **Jennifer Robles**, Ventura Unified School District, CA; **Priscilla Rocha**, Clark County School District, NV; **Dzidra Rodins**, DePaul University IL; **Maria Rodriguez**, Central High School, AZ; **Maria Ruiz**, Victor Valley College, CA; **Kimberly Russell**, Clark College, WA; **Irene Sakk**, Northwestern University, IL; **Shaeley Santiago**, Ames High School, IA; **Peg Sarosy**, San Francisco State University, CA; **Alice Savage**, North Harris College, TX; **Donna Schaeffer**, University of Washington, WA; **Carol Schinger**, Northern Virginia Community College, VA; **Robert Scott**, Kansas State University, KS; **Suell Scott**, Sheridan Technical Center, FL; **Shira Seaman**, Global English Academy, NY; **Richard Seltzer**, Glendale Community College, CA; **Kathy Sherak**, San Francisco State University, CA; **German Silva**, Miami Dade College, FL; **Andrea Spector**, Santa Monica Community College, CA; **Karen Stanley**, Central Piedmont Community College, NC; **Ayse Stromsdorfer**, Soldan I.S.H.S., MO; **Yilin Sun**, South Seattle Community College, WA; **Thomas Swietlik**, Intrax International Institute, IL; **Judith Tanka**, UCLA Extension–American Language Center, CA; **Priscilla Taylor**, University of Southern California, CA; **Ilene Teixeira**, Fairfax County Public Schools, VA; **Shirl H. Terrell**, Collin College, TX; **Marya Teutsch-Dwyer**, St. Cloud State University, MN; **Stephen Thergesen**, ELS Language Centers, CO; **Christine Tierney**, Houston Community College, TX; **Arlene Turini**, North Moore High School, NC; **Suzanne Van Der Valk**, Iowa State University, IA; **Nathan D. Vasarhely**, Ygnacio Valley High School, CA; **Naomi S. Verratti**, Howard Community College, MD; **Hollyahna Vettori**, Santa Rosa Junior College, CA; **Julie Vorholt**, Lewis & Clark College, OR; **Laura Walsh**, City College of San Francisco, CA; **Andrew J. Watson**, The English Bakery; **Donald Weasenforth**, Collin College, TX; **Juliane Widner**, Sheepshead Bay High School, NY; **Lynne Wilkins**, Mills College, CA; **Dolores "Lorrie" Winter**, California State University at Fullerton, CA; **Jody Yamamoto**, Kapi'olani Community College, HI; **Ellen L. Yaniv**, Boston University, MA; **Norman Yoshida**, Lewis & Clark College, OR; **Joanna Zadra**, American River College, CA; **Florence Zysman**, Santiago Canyon College, CA;

ASIA **Rabiatu Abubakar**, Eton Language Centre, Malaysia; **Wiwik Andreani**, Bina Nusantara University, Indonesia; **Mike Baker**, Kosei Junior High School, Japan; **Leonard Barrow**, Kanto Junior College, Japan; **Herman Bartelen**, Japan; **Siren Betty**, Fooyin University, Kaohsiung; **Thomas E. Bieri**, Nagoya College, Japan; **Natalie Brezden**, Global English House, Japan; **MK Brooks**, Mukogawa Women's University, Japan; **Truong Ngoc Buu**, The Youth Language School, Vietnam; **Charles Cabell**, Toyo University, Japan; **Fred Carruth**, Matsumoto University, Japan; **Frances Causer**, Seijo University, Japan; **Deborah Chang**, Wenzao Ursuline College of Languages, Kaohsiung; **David Chatham**, Ritsumeikan University, Japan; **Andrew Chih Hong Chen**, National Sun Yat-sen University, Kaohsiung; **Christina Chen**, Yu-Tsai Bilingual Elementary School, Taipei; **Jason Jeffree Cole**, Coto College, Japan; **Le Minh Cong**, Vungtau Tourism Vocational College, Vietnam; **Todd Cooper**, Toyama National College of Technology, Japan; **Marie Cosgrove**, Daito Bunka University, Japan; **Tony Cripps**, Ritsumeikan University, Japan; **Daniel Cussen**, Takushoku University, Japan; **Le Dan**, Ho Chi Minh City Electric Power College, Vietnam; **Simon Daykin**, Banghwa-dong Community Centre, South Korea; **Aimee Denham**, ILA, Vietnam; **Bryan Dickson**, David's English Center, Taipei; **Nathan Ducker**, Japan University, Japan; **Ian Duncan**, Simul International Corporate Training, Japan; **Nguyen Thi Kieu Dung**, Thang Long University, Vietnam; **Nguyen Thi Thuy Duong**, Vietnamese American Vocational Training College, Vietnam; **Wong Tuck Ee**, Raja Tun Azlan Science Secondary School, Malaysia; **Emilia Effendy**, International Islamic University Malaysia, Malaysia; **Robert Eva**, Kaisei Girls High School, Japan; **Jim George**, Luna International Language School, Japan; **Jurgen Germeys**, Silk Road Language Center, South Korea; **Wong Ai Gnoh**, SMJK Chung Hwa Confucian, Malaysia; **Peter Gosselink**, Hokkai High School,

Japan; **Wendy M. Gough**, St. Mary College/Nunoike Gaigo Senmon Gakko, Japan; **Tim Grose**, Sapporo Gakuin University, Japan; **Pham Thu Ha**, Le Van Tam Primary School, Vietnam; **Ann-Marie Hadzima**, Taipei; **Troy Hammond**, Tokyo Gakugei University International Secondary School, Japan; **Robiatul 'Adawiah Binti Hamzah**, SMK Putrajaya Precinct 8(1), Malaysia; **Tran Thi Thuy Hang**, Ho Chi Minh City Banking University, Vietnam; **To Thi Hong Hanh**, CEFALT, Vietnam; **Janis Hearn**, Hongik University, South Korea; **David Hindman**, Sejong University, South Korea; **Nahn Cam Hoa**, Ho Chi Minh City University of Technology, Vietnam; **Jana Holt**, Korea University, South Korea; **Jason Hollowell**, Nihon University, Japan; **F. N. (Zoe) Hsu**, National Tainan University, Yong Kang; **Wenhua Hsu**, I-Shou University, Kaohsiung; **Luu Nguyen Quoc Hung**, Cantho University, Vietnam; **Cecile Hwang**, Changwon National University, South Korea; **Ainol Haryati Ibrahim**, Universiti Malaysia Pahang, Malaysia; **Robert Jeens**, Yonsei University, South Korea; **Linda M. Joyce**, Kyushu Sangyo University, Japan; **Dr. Nisai Kaewsanchai**, English Square Kanchanaburi, Thailand; **Aniza Kamarulzaman**, Sabah Science Secondary School, Malaysia; **Ikuko Kashiwabara**, Osaka Electro-Communication University, Japan; **Gurmit Kaur**, INTI College, Malaysia; **Nick Keane**, Japan; **Ward Ketcheson**, Aomori University, Japan; **Montchatry Ketmuni**, Rajamangala University of Technology, Thailand; **Dinh Viet Khanh**, Vietnam; **Seonok Kim**, Kangsu Jongro Language School, South Korea; **Kelly P. Kimura**, Soka University, Japan; **Stan Kirk**, Konan University, Japan; **Donald Knight**, Nan Hua/Fu Li Junior High Schools, Hsinchu; **Kari J. Kostiainen**, Nagoya City University, Japan; **Pattri Kuanpulpol**, Silpakorn University, Thailand; **Ha Thi Lan**, Thai Binh Teacher Training College, Vietnam; **Eric Edwin Larson**, Miyazaki Prefectural Nursing University, Japan; **Richard S. Lavin**, Prefectural University of Kumamoto, Japan; **Shirley Leane**, Chugoku Junior College, Japan; **Tae Lee**, Yonsei University, South Korea; **Lys Yongsoon Lee**, Reading Town Geumcheon, South Korea; **Mallory Leece**, Sun Moon University, South Korea; **Dang Hong Lien**, Tan Lam Upper Secondary School, Vietnam; **Huang Li-Han**, Rebecca Education Institute, Taipei; **Sovannarith Lim**, Royal University of Phnom Penh, Cambodia; **Ginger Lin**, National Kaohsiung Hospitality College, Kaohsiung; **Noel Lineker**, New Zealand/Japan; **Tran Dang Khanh Linh**, Nha Trang Teachers' Training College, Vietnam; **Daphne Liu**, Buliton English School, Taipei; **S. F. Josephine Liu**, Tien-Mu Elementary School, Taipei; **Caroline Luo**, Tunghai University, Taichung; **Jeng-Jia Luo**, Tunghai University, Taichung; **Laura MacGregor**, Gakushuin University, Japan; **Amir Madani**, Visuttharangsi School, Thailand; **Elena Maeda**, Sacred Heart Professional Training College, Japan; **Vu Thi Thanh Mai**, Hoang Gia Education Center, Vietnam; **Kimura Masakazu**, Kato Gakuen Gyoshu High School, Japan; **Susumu Matsuhashi**, Net Link English School, Japan; **James McCrostie**, Daito Bunka University, Japan; **Joel McKee**, Inha University, South Korea; **Colin McKenzie**, Wachirawit Primary School, Thailand; **William K. Moore**, Hiroshima Kokusai Gakuin University, Japan; **Hudson Murrell**, Baiko Gakuin University, Japan; **Frances Namba**, Senri International School of Kwansei Gakuin, Japan; **Keiichi Narita**, Niigata University, Japan; **Kim Chung Nguyen**, Ho Chi Minh University of Industry, Vietnam; **Do Thi Thanh Nhan**, Hanoi University, Vietnam; **Dale Kazuo Nishi**, Aoyama English Conversation School, Japan; **Louise Ohashi**, Shukutoku University, Japan; **Virginia Peng**, Ritsumeikan University, Japan; **Suangkanok Piboonthamnont**, Rajamangala University of Technology, Thailand; **Simon Pitcher**, Business English Teaching Services, Japan; **John C. Probert**, New Education Worldwide, Thailand; **Do Thi Hoa Quyen**, Ton Duc Thang University, Vietnam; **John P. Racine**, Dokkyo University, Japan; **Kevin Ramsden**, Kyoto University of Foreign Studies, Japan; **Luis Rappaport**, Cung Thieu Nha Ha Noi, Vietnam; **Lisa Reshad**, Konan Daigaku Hyogo, Japan; **Peter Riley**, Taisho University, Japan; **Thomas N. Robb**, Kyoto Sangyo University, Japan; **Maria Feti Rosyani**, Universitas Kristen Indonesia, Indonesia; **Greg Rouault**, Konan University, Japan; **Chris Ruddenklau**, Kindai University, Japan; **Hans-Gustav Schwartz**, Thailand; **Mary-Jane Scott**, Soongsil University, South Korea; **Jenay Seymour**, Hongik University, South Korea; **James Sherlock**, A.P.W. Angthong, Thailand; **Yuko Shimizu**, Ritsumeikan University, Japan; **Suzila Mohd Shukor**, Universiti Sains Malaysia, Malaysia; **Stephen E. Smith**, Mahidol University, Thailand; **Mi-young Song**, Kyungwon University, South Korea; **Jason Stewart**, Taejon International Language School, South Korea; **Brian A. Stokes**, Korea University, South Korea; **Mulder Su**, Shih-Chien University, Kaohsiung;

Yoomi Suh, English Plus, South Korea; **Yun-Fang Sun**, Wenzao Ursuline College of Languages, Kaohsiung; **Richard Swingle**, Kansai Gaidai University, Japan; **Tran Hoang Tan**, School of International Training, Vietnam; **Takako Tanaka**, Doshisha University, Japan; **Jeffrey Taschner**, American University Alumni Language Center, Thailand ; **Michael Taylor**, International Pioneers School, Thailand; **Tran Duong The**, Sao Mai Language Center, Vietnam; **Tran Dinh Tho**, Duc Tri Secondary School, Vietnam; **Huynh Thi Anh Thu**, Nhatrang College of Culture Arts and Tourism, Vietnam; **Peter Timmins**, Peter's English School, Japan; **Fumie Togano**, Hosei Daini High School, Japan; **F. Sigmund Topor**, Keio University Language School, Japan; **Yen-Cheng Tseng**, Chang-Jung Christian University, Tainan; **Hajime Uematsu**, Hirosaki University, Japan; **Rachel Um**, Mok-dong Oedae English School, South Korea; **David Underhill**, EEExpress, Japan; **Siriluck Usaha**, Sripatum University, Thailand; **Tyas Budi Utami**, Indonesia; **Nguyen Thi Van**, Far East International School, Vietnam; **Stephan Van Eycken**, Kosei Gakuen Girls High School, Japan; **Zisa Velasquez**, Taihu International School/Semarang International School, China/Indonesia; **Jeffrey Walter**, Sangji University, South Korea; **Bill White**, Kinki University, Japan; **Yohanes De Deo Widyastoko**, Xaverius Senior High School, Indonesia; **Greg Chung-Hsien Wu**, Providence University, Taichung; **Hui-Lien Yeh**, Chai Nan University of Pharmacy and Science, Tainan; **Sittiporn Yodnil**, Huachiew Chalermprakiet University, Thailand; **Ming-Yu Li**, Chang-Jung, Christian University, Tainan; **Shamshul Helmy Zambahari**, Universiti Teknologi Malaysia, Malaysia; **Aimin Fadhlee bin Mahmud Zuhodi**, Kuala Terengganu Science School, Malaysia

TURKEY **Gül Akkoç**, Boğaziçi University; **Seval Akmeşe**, Haliç University; **Deniz Balım**, Haliç University; **Robert Ledbury**, Izmir University of Economics; **Oya Özağaç**, Boğaziçi University

THE MIDDLE EAST **Amina Saif Mohammed Al Hashamia**, Nizwa College of Applied Sciences, Oman; **Sharon Ruth Devaneson**, Ibri College of Technology, Oman; **Hanaa El-Deeb**, Canadian International College, Egypt; **Brian Gay**, Sultan Qaboos University, Oman; **Gail Al-Hafidh**, Sharjah Higher Colleges of Technology, U.A.E.; **Jonathan Hastings**, American Language Center, Jordan; **Sian Khoury**, Fujairah Women's College (HCT), U.A.E.; **Jessica March**, American University of Sharjah, U.A.E.; **Neil McBeath**, Sultan Qaboos University, Oman

LATIN AMERICA **Aldana Aguirre**, Argentina; **Claudia Almeida**, Coordenação de Idiomas, Brazil; **Cláudia Arias**, Brazil; **Maria de los Angeles Barba**, FES Acatlan UNAM, Mexico; **Lilia Barrios**, Universidad Autónoma de Tamaulipas, Mexico; **Adán Beristain**, UAEM, Mexico; **Ricardo Böck**, Manoel Ribas, Brazil; **Edson Braga**, CNA, Brazil; **Marli Buttelli**, Mater et Magistra, Brazil; **Alessandra Campos**, Inova Centro de Linguas, Brazil; **Priscila Catta Preta Ribeiro**, Brazil; **Gustavo Cestari**, Access International School, Brazil; **Walter D'Alessandro**, Virginia Language Center, Brazil; **Lilian De Gennaro**, Argentina; **Mônica De Stefani**, Quality Centro de Idiomas, Brazil; **Julio Alejandro Flores**, BUAP, Mexico; **Mirian Freire**, CNA Vila Guilherme, Brazil; **Francisco Garcia**, Colegio Lestonnac de San Angel, Mexico; **Miriam Giovanardi**, Brazil; **Darlene Gonzalez Miy**, ITESM CCV, Mexico; **Maria Laura Grimaldi**, Argentina; **Luz Dary Guzmán**, IMPAHU, Colombia; **Carmen Koppe**, Brazil; **Monica Krutzler**, Brazil; **Marcus Murilo Lacerda**, Seven Idiomas, Brazil; **Nancy Lake**, CEL-LEP, Brazil; **Cris Lazzerini**, Brazil; **Sandra Luna**, Argentina; **Ricardo Luvisan**, Brazil; **Jorge Murilo Menezes**, ACBEU, Brazil; **Monica Navarro**, Instituto Cultural A. C., Mexico; **Joacyr Oliveira**, Faculdades Metropolitanas Unidas and Summit School for Teachers, Brazil; **Ayrton Cesar Oliveira de Araujo**, E&A English Classes, Brazil; **Ana Laura Oriente**, Seven Idiomas, Brazil; **Adelia Peña Clavel**, CELE UNAM, Mexico; **Beatriz Pereira**, Summit School, Brazil; **Miguel Perez**, Instituto Cultural Mexico; **Cristiane Perone**, Associação Cultura Inglesa, Brazil; **Pamela Claudia Pogré**, Colegio Integral Caballito/ Universidad de Flores, Argentina; **Dalva Prates**, Brazil; **Marianne Rampaso**, Iowa Idiomas, Brazil; **Daniela Rutolo**, Instituto Superior Cultural Británico, Argentina; **Maione Sampaio**, Maione Carrijo Consultoria em Inglês Ltda, Brazil; **Elaine Santesso**, TS Escola de Idiomas, Brazil; **Camila Francisco Santos**, UNS Idiomas, Brazil; **Lucia Silva**, Cooplem Idiomas, Brazil; **Maria Adela Sorzio**, Instituto Superior Santa Cecilia, Argentina; **Elcio Souza**, Unibero, Brazil; **Willie Thomas**, Rainbow Idiomas, Brazil; **Sandra Villegas**, Instituto Humberto de Paolis, Argentina; **John Whelan**, La Universidad Nacional Autonoma de Mexico, Mexico

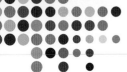

WELCOME TO Q:Skills for Success

**Q: Skills for Success is a six-level series with two strands,
Reading and Writing and *Listening and Speaking*.**

READING AND WRITING

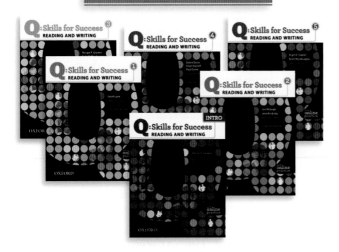

LISTENING AND SPEAKING

WITH Q ONLINE PRACTICE

STUDENT AND TEACHER INFORMED

Q: Skills for Success is the result of an extensive development process involving thousands
of teachers and hundreds of students around the world. Their views and opinions helped
shape the content of the series. *Q* is grounded in teaching theory as well as real-world
classroom practice, making it the most learner-centered series available.

CONTENTS

Q connects critical thinking, language skills, and learning outcomes.

LANGUAGE SKILLS

Explicit skills instruction enables students to meet their academic and professional goals.

LEARNING OUTCOMES

Clearly identified **learning outcomes** focus students on the goal of their instruction.

UNIT **4**

Food

READING	scanning for information
VOCABULARY	using the dictionary
GRAMMAR	verbs + gerunds or infinitives
WRITING	writing complete sentences

LEARNING OUTCOME

Describe the people, food, and activities at a celebration.

Unit QUESTION

When do we eat special foods?

PREVIEW THE UNIT

A Answer the questions. Then share your answers with a partner.

1. What snacks do you like to eat? What is your favorite dinner? What is your favorite dessert?

2. Why do you usually eat? Check (✓) the boxes.

I eat because . . .

□ I'm hungry.   □ it's fun to do with friends.
□ it's time for a meal.   □ I like to be with my family.
□ I'm bored.

B Look at the photo. Who are the people? What are they doing?

C Discuss the Unit Question above with your classmates.

Listen to *The Q Classroom*, Track 8, to hear other answers.

48   UNIT 4

49

CRITICAL THINKING

Thought-provoking **unit questions** engage students with the topic and provide a **critical thinking framework** for the unit.

> Having the learning outcome is important because it gives students and teachers a clear idea of what the point of each task/activity in the unit is.
> *Lawrence Lawson, Palomar College, California*

((•)) Track 9   **Read the article.**

LANGUAGE SKILLS

Reading texts provide input on the unit question and give **exposure to academic content.**

Celebrating the New Year with Food

1   The New Year is a very **special** occasion. We say goodbye to the last year, and we think about the future. We **celebrate** with family members, friends, and neighbors. **Cultures** around the world celebrate the New Year, but everyone celebrates it a little differently. For everyone, New Year's means special food.

Chinese New Year Cake

making Vietnamese rice cake

2   In many parts of the world, rice is the most important **ingredient** in New Year's

foods. People **prepare** rice in many different ways—from rice cakes to rice soup. In Korea, parents encourage children to eat all of their rice cake soup for a good year. In Vietnam, people carefully wrap a rice cake in a large, **fresh** green leaf. This makes a perfect square cake. In China, the New Year Cake is a special sweet cake with rice. Every area of China has a different kind of New Year Cake.

3   In other parts of the world, beans are the common ingredients in many New

CRITICAL THINKING

Students **discuss** their opinions of each reading text and **analyze** how it changes their perspective on the unit question.

Q? **WHAT DO YOU THINK?**

A. Write your favorite celebration in the chart. It can [ ] anniversary, or holiday. Answer the questions.

	My favorite celebration	My partner's favorite celebration
1. When do you usually have this celebration?		

 One of the best features is your focus on developing materials of a high "interest level."

Troy Hammond, Tokyo Gakugei University,
International Secondary School, Japan

Explicit skills instruction prepares students for academic success.

Writing Skill | **Writing complete sentences**

Every sentence needs a **subject** and a **verb**. The **subject** is a noun or pronoun. It answers the question "Who or what is the sentence about?" The **verb** is the action. It answers the question "What does the subject do, think, or feel?"

I prepare dinner every day.
subject verb

Usually my dinners are delicious.
subject verb

My friends like to go to cafés.
subject verb

Right now, they are at a café.
subject verb

Always make your subject and verb agree.

✓ Correct: I like oranges.   ←   Subject and verb agree.
✓ Correct: He likes oranges.   ←   Subject and verb agree.
✗ Incorrect: He like oranges.   ←   Subject and verb do not agree.

Tip for Success

When a sentence has two clauses (parts) joined by *because* or *and*, each clause must have a subject and a verb. *I like cake because it is sweet.*

A. Add a subject (*he, she, it,* or *they*) or the verb *be* to each sentence.

1. My brother _is_ a student in a cooking program.
2. Is a very difficult book.
3. There delicious dishes on this menu.
4. Are very good cookies.
5. Is an excellent baker.
6. Kate at the café this afternoon.
7. I rarely eat seafood because it usually very expensive.
8. Carlos likes to eat in restaurants because doesn't like cooking.

B. Correct the incorrect verb in each sentence.

1. Sam _goes_ go to the cafeteria after class.
2. Mary have a new job as a waitress.
3. They loves to eat popcorn at the movie theater.
4. Hassan prepare coffee every morning.
5. I are at the same table as my friends.

in a supermarket

A. Complete the sentences. Use verb + gerund or verb + infinitive.

1. Every week, I _____ need to buy _____ (need / buy) food at the supermarket.
2. Sam is heavy, so he _____ (avoid / eat) candy.
3. I _____ (try / eat) lunch every day, but sometimes I don't have time.
4. Toshi _____ (hate / cook), but he washes the dishes after dinner.
5. Anna _____ (hate / wash) dishes.
6. My classmates _____ (enjoy / have) coffee together after class.
7. My neighbor _____ (love / watch) cooking programs on TV.
8. My cousin _____ (want / be) a famous cook on TV.

B. Answer the questions. Use verb + infinitive or verb + gerund.

1. What do you like to eat for breakfast?
   _____

2. What foods do you like to prepare?
   _____

3. What vegetable do you hate eating?
   _____

4. What snack do you enjoy eating with your friends?
   _____

5. What foods do you avoid eating?
   _____

 The tasks are simple, accessible, user-friendly, and very useful.
Jessica March, American University of Sharjah, U.A.E.

Q Online Practice provides all new content for additional practice in an easy-to-use online workbook. Every student book includes a *Q Online Practice access code card*. Use the access code to register for your *Q Online Practice* account at www.Qonlinepractice.com.

Building Vocabulary | **Using the dictionary** | web⁺

You can build your vocabulary by **using the dictionary**. Look at the entry

> **fruit** 🔑 /frut/ *noun* [count, noncount]
>
> ⓘ **PRONUNCIATION**
> The word **fruit** sounds like **boot**.
>
> the part of a plant or tree that holds the seeds. Oranges and apples are types of **fruit**: *Would you like **a piece of fruit**? •* "*Would you like **some** fruit?*" "*Yes please – I'll have a pear.*"

Use the dictionary entry to learn new words. In this definition for *fruit*, you can learn other important words: *plant*, *tree*, and *seeds*. You learn that oranges, apples, and pears are types of fruit. In addition, many learners' dictionaries have color illustrations to show vocabulary.

All dictionary entries are from the *Oxford Basic American Dictionary for learners of English* © Oxford University Press 2011.

LANGUAGE SKILLS

A **research-based vocabulary program** focuses students on the words they need to know academically and professionally, using skill strategies based on the same research as the Oxford dictionaries.

Your key to building English language skills **NEW**

Oxford
Basic
AMERICAN
DICTIONARY | for learners of English

with interactive dictionary on CD-ROM

All dictionary entries are taken from the *Oxford Basic American Dictionary for learners of English*.

The *Oxford Basic American Dictionary for learners of English* was designed with English learners in mind, and provides extra learning tools for pronunciation, verb types, basic grammar structures, and more.

The Oxford 2000 Keywords 🔑
The Oxford 2000 keywords encompasses the **2000 most important words to learn in English**. It is based on a comprehensive analysis of the Oxford English Corpus, a two-billion-word collection of English text, and on extensive research with both language and pedagogical experts.

The Academic Word List AWL
The Academic Word List was created by Averil Coxhead and contains **570 words that are commonly used in academic English**, such as in textbooks or articles across a wide range of academic subject areas. These words are a great place to start if you are studying English for academic purposes.

Clear learning outcomes focus students on the goals of instruction.

LEARNING OUTCOMES

A culminating unit assignment evaluates the students' **mastery of the learning outcome.**

Unit Assignment | **Describe a special meal or celebration**

In this assignment, you describe a special meal or celebration. Think about the Unit Question, "When do we eat special foods?" and use the Self-Assessment checklist on page 60.

A. BRAINSTORM Look at the categories in the idea map below. Then draw an idea map in your notebook. Complete the map with words about a special meal or celebration. Then explain your map to a partner.

When?   Where?   Why?

Special meal or celebration

LEARNER CENTERED

Track Your Success allows students to **assess their own progress** and provides guidance on remediation.

Check (✓) the skills you learned. If you need more work on a skill, refer to the page(s) in parentheses.

READING	I can scan for information. (p. 53)
VOCABULARY	I can use the dictionary to build my vocabulary. (p. 53)
GRAMMAR	I can use verbs with gerunds and infinitives. (p. 56)
WRITING	I can write complete sentences. (p. 58)
LEARNING OUTCOME	I can describe the people, food, and activities at a celebration. (p. 59)

Students can check their learning ... and they can focus on the essential points when they study.

Suh Yoomi, Seoul, South Korea

Q Online Practice

For the student

- **Easy-to-use:** a simple interface allows students to focus on enhancing their reading and writing skills, not learning a new software program
- **Flexible:** for use anywhere there's an Internet connection
- **Access code card:** a *Q Online Practice* access code is included with this book—use the access code to register for *Q Online Practice* at www.Qonlinepractice.com

For the teacher

- **Simple yet powerful:** automatically grades student exercises and tracks progress
- **Straightforward:** online management system to review, print, or export reports
- **Flexible:** for use in the classroom or easily assigned as homework
- **Access code card:** with the *Q Teacher's Handbook* or sold separately

Teacher Resources

Q Teacher's Handbook gives strategic support through:

- specific teaching notes for each activity
- ideas for ensuring student participation
- multilevel strategies and expansion activities
- the answer key
- special sections on 21st century skills and critical thinking
- a *Testing Program CD-ROM* with a customizable test for each unit
- a *Q Online Practice* teacher's access code card

Oxford Teachers' Club

For additional resources visit the
Q: Skills for Success companion website at
www.oup.com/elt/teacher/Qskillsforsuccess

Q Class Audio includes:

- reading texts
- *The Q Classroom*

It's an interesting, engaging series which provides plenty of materials that are easy to use in class, as well as instructionally promising.
Donald Weasenforth, Collin College, Texas

UNIT	READING	WRITING
1 People **What kind of person are you?** READING: What Kind of Person Are You? A Magazine Article (Social Psychology)	• Identify topics and main ideas • Preview text using a variety of strategies • Read for main ideas • Read for details • Read and recognize different text types	• Write answers to questions in complete sentences • Plan before writing • Make an outline • Revise, edit, and rewrite • Give feedback to peers and self-assess
2 Friendship **Who are your friends?** READING: Different Kinds of Friends A Web Article (Relationships)	• Preview text using a variety of strategies • Read for main ideas • Read for details • Identifying topics and main ideas • Read and recognize different text types	• Edit for capitalization and punctuation • Make idea maps • Brainstorm ideas • Revise, edit, and rewrite • Give feedback to peers and self-assess
3 Education **Do students spend too much time in school?** READING: Comparing Schools in Three Countries A Magazine Article (Education)	• Scanning for names, dates, and times • Preview text using a variety of strategies • Read for main ideas • Read for details • Read and recognize different text types	• Use capitalization and punctuation correctly • Plan before writing • Revise, edit, and rewrite • Edit your writing • Give feedback to peers and self-assess
4 Food **When do we eat special foods?** READING: Celebrating the New Year with Food A Magazine Article (Food and Culture)	• Preview text using a variety of strategies • Scan for information • Read for main ideas • Read for details • Read and recognize different text types	• Write complete sentences • Use subject-verb agreement • Plan before writing • Use an idea map • Revise, edit, and rewrite • Give feedback to peers and self-assess

VOCABULARY	GRAMMAR	CRITICAL THINKING	UNIT OUTCOME
• Use descriptive adjectives • Match definitions • Match opposites • Define new terms • Learn selected vocabulary words from the Oxford 2000 and the Academic Word List	• Present of *be*; simple present affirmative statements	• Use lists to demonstrate knowledge • Apply knowledge to complete a new task • Reflect on the unit question • Connect ideas across texts or readings • Express ideas/reactions/opinions orally and in writing • Apply unit tips and use *Q Online Practice* to become a strategic learner	• Write sentences to describe your personality, appearance, and interests.
• Use word families to expand vocabulary • Identify parts of speech • Match definitions • Define new terms • Learn selected vocabulary words from the Oxford 2000 and the Academic Word List	• Simple present	• Use a chart to understand concepts and identify patterns • Classify information • Reflect on the unit question • Connect ideas across texts or readings • Express ideas/reactions/opinions orally and in writing • Apply unit tips and use *Q Online Practice* to become a strategic learner	• Write complete sentences about three friends using descriptive adjectives.
• Use a vocabulary log to remember new words • Match definitions • Define new terms • Learn selected vocabulary words from the Oxford 2000 and the Academic Word List	• Adjectives; adverbs + adjectives	• Recognize information to show you understand and remember • Use a chart to organize information • Reflect on the unit question • Connect ideas across texts or readings • Express ideas/reactions/opinions orally and in writing • Apply unit tips and use *Q Online Practice* to become a strategic learner	• Give information about a school using descriptive adjectives and adverbs.
• Use examples in a dictionary to learn related words • Match definitions • Define new terms • Learn selected vocabulary words from the Oxford 2000 and the Academic Word List	• Verbs + gerunds or infinitives	• Locate information in a text • Classify ideas using a chart • Reflect on the unit question • Connect ideas across texts or readings • Express ideas/reactions/opinions orally and in writing • Apply unit tips and practice *Q* online to become a strategic learner	• Describe the people, food, and activities at a celebration.

UNIT	READING	WRITING
5 Fun **How do you have fun?** **READING: No Money? Have Fun Anyway!** Web Posts (Entertainment)	• Underline and highlight to note important information • Preview text using a variety of strategies • Read for main ideas • Read for details • Read and recognize different text types	• Plan before writing • Use a chart to generate ideas • Write complete sentences • Revise, edit, and rewrite • Give feedback to peers and self-assess
6 Home **What is your favorite room?** **READING 1: There's No Place Like Home** A Web Article (Design) **READING 2: A Tall Man in a Small Space** A Newspaper Article (Design)	• Preview text using a variety of strategies • Underline and highlight to note important information • Read for main ideas • Read for details • Read and recognize different text types	• Write a paragraph using a topic sentence, supporting sentences, and a concluding sentence • Plan before writing • Use visuals to generate ideas • Revise, edit, and rewrite • Give feedback to peers and self-assess
7 Weather **Where is the best and the worst weather?** **READING 1: Good Weather, Bad Weather** A Web Article (Weather and Geography) **READING 2: Storm Chasers!** A Web Article (Careers)	• Identify pronoun references • Locate information in a text • Preview text using a variety of strategies • Read for main ideas • Read for details • Read and recognize different text types	• Plan before writing • Make an outline • Write a paragraph using a topic sentence, supporting sentences, and a concluding sentence • Revise, edit, and rewrite • Give feedback to peers and self-assess
8 Health **How can you change an unhealthy habit?** **READING 1: When Does a Change Become a Habit?** A Magazine Article (Psychology) **READING 2: Dr. Lee on Health** A Newspaper Article (Behavior and Health)	• Scan for information • Preview text using a variety of strategies • Read for main ideas • Read for details • Identify pronoun references • Read and recognize different text types	• Support ideas with examples and/or reasons • Use appropriate connectors to convey ideas • Write a paragraph • Plan before writing • Revise, edit, and rewrite • Give feedback to peers and self-assess

VOCABULARY	GRAMMAR	CRITICAL THINKING	UNIT OUTCOME
• Use verb + noun collocations • Match definitions • Define new terms • Learn selected vocabulary words from the Oxford 2000 and the Academic Word List	• Subject and object pronouns	• Highlight or underline to understand the difference between important information and supporting details • Reflect on the unit question • Connect ideas across texts or readings • Express ideas/reactions/ opinions orally and in writing • Apply unit tips and use *Q Online Practice* to become a strategic learner	• Explain what you do for fun and why you enjoy it.
• Use word categories to expand vocabulary • Match definitions • Define new terms • Learn selected vocabulary words from the Oxford 2000 and the Academic Word List	• Prepositions of location	• Categorize information to see similarities and differences • Reflect on the unit question • Connect ideas across texts or readings • Express ideas/reactions/ opinions orally and in writing • Apply unit tips and use *Q Online Practice* to become a strategic learner	• Write a paragraph describing your favorite room using prepositions.
• Use the dictionary to find synonyms • Match definitions • Define new terms • Learn selected vocabulary words from the Oxford 2000 and the Academic Word List	• Adverbs of frequency	• Show understanding of the connection between pronouns and the nouns to follow ideas • Reflect on the unit question • Connect ideas across texts or readings • Express ideas/reactions/ opinions orally and in writing • Apply unit tips and use *Q Online Practice* to become a strategic learner	• Write a paragraph describing types of weather in answer to a question prompt.
• Use verb + noun and verb + preposition collocations • Match definitions • Define new terms • Learn selected vocabulary words from the Oxford 2000 and the Academic Word List	• Modals *can*, *could*, and *should*	• Transfer knowledge to use it in a new way • Support ideas with examples and reasons • Reflect on the unit question • Connect ideas across texts or readings • Express ideas/reactions/ opinions orally and in writing • Apply unit tips and use *Q Online Practice* to become a strategic learner	• Write a paragraph about how to change a bad habit.

UNIT	READING	WRITING
9 Cities **Q** **Why do people live in cities?** **READING 1: Why Do People Love Their Cities?** A Magazine Article (Urban Planning) **READING 2: First Impressions** A Web Article (Sociology)	• Build reading fluency • Preview text using a variety of strategies • Locate information in a text • Distinguish between main ideas and supporting ideas • Read for main ideas • Read for details • Read and recognize different text types	• Write two paragraphs • Plan before writing • Use a T-chart to generate ideas • Support ideas • Revise, edit, and rewrite • Give feedback to peers and self-assess
10 Milestones **Q** **What events change our lives?** **READING 1: A Promise to Children** A Magazine Article (Education and Development) **READING 2: An Extraordinary Coach** A Magazine Article (Sports and Leadership)	• Preview text using a variety of strategies • Build reading fluency • Read for main ideas • Read for details • Read and recognize different text types	• Show the sequence of events • Write a paragraph about an important event in your life • Plan before writing • Make a timeline to organize ideas • Revise, edit, and rewrite • Give feedback to peers and self-assess

VOCABULARY	GRAMMAR	CRITICAL THINKING	UNIT OUTCOME
• Use the dictionary to find other words in the same word families • Match definitions • Define new terms • Learn selected vocabulary words from the Oxford 2000 and the Academic Word List	• Past of *be*; simple past affirmative statements	• Use charts to make connections • Reflect on the unit question • Connect ideas across texts or readings • Express ideas/reactions/opinions orally and in writing • Apply unit tips and use *Q Online Practice* to become a strategic learner	• Write two paragraphs describing a city you visited.
• Use the dictionary to find correct definitions • Match definitions • Define new terms • Learn selected vocabulary words from the Oxford 2000 and the Academic Word List	• Simple past with regular and irregular verbs	• Make a timeline to sequence events • Reflect on the unit question • Connect ideas across texts or readings • Express ideas/reactions/opinions orally and in writing • Apply unit tips and use *Q Online Practice* to become a strategic learner	• Write a paragraph about an important event in your life.

READING   ●   identifying topics and main ideas

VOCABULARY   ●   descriptive adjectives

GRAMMAR   ●   present of *be*; simple present affirmative statements

Write sentences to describe your personality, appearance, and interests.

Unit QUESTION

What kind of person are you?

PREVIEW THE UNIT

A Circle a word or fill in the blank to complete each statement. Then compare with a partner.

1. I am (friendly / quiet).

2. I am (tall / short).

3. I like (sports / movies / school).

4. I am good at (math / English / history).

5. My friends say I am _____.

6. I think I am _____.

B Look at the photo. How do you think these people are different? Why?

C Discuss the Unit Question above with your classmates.

Listen to *The Q Classroom*, Track 2, to hear other answers.

READING | What Kind of Person Are You?

VOCABULARY

A. Here are some words from the Reading. Read the sentences. Which explanation is correct? Circle *a* or *b*.

Sam is outgoing.

Anna is fashionable.

June is messy.

1. Please **describe** your brother. Is he tall? What color is his hair?
   a. Help your brother.
   b. Tell me about your brother.

2. Sam is very **outgoing**. He likes to meet new people, and he has many friends.
   a. Sam is friendly.
   b. Sam is quiet.

3. Sarah is very **talkative**. She talks to everyone!
   a. Sarah talks a lot.
   b. Sarah talks very little.

4. Rob has a nice **personality**. He's very kind and helpful.
   a. Rob acts in a nice way.
   b. Rob has a nice name.

5. Anna is very **fashionable**. She always wears nice, new clothes.
   a. Anna doesn't care about clothes.
   b. Anna likes clothes and she dresses well.

6. June's room is **messy**. There are books and clothes everywhere.
   a. June's room is clean.
   b. June's room is not clean.

7. Toshi is not very tall and not very short. He is **average** height.
   a. Toshi's height is normal.
   b. Toshi's height is not normal.

8. John is a **serious** person. He almost never laughs.
   a. John is happy, and he's a funny person.
   b. John is quiet, and he's not funny.

B. Complete the sentences with the words from Activity A. (You will not use all the words.)

1. I'm not thin and I'm not heavy. My weight is about _____.

2. Can you _____ your brother? What does he look like?

3. My boots are ten years old. They aren't very _____.

4. She is a(n) _____ person. She talks to everyone.

5. Mary is shy. She has a quiet _____.

6. Don't be _____ all the time. Have some fun!

Tip for Success

Before you read a text, look at the title. Then look at the pictures. What do they tell you about the reading?

PREVIEW THE READING

This magazine article describes different kinds of people. Look quickly at the article. Find words to describe people. Circle the words.

Track 3   **Read the article.**

What Kind of Person Are You?

This week, *Talk Magazine* is asking people about themselves. Read each question and the two answers. Which answer **describes** you? Check (✓) one name in each pair.

1. **Are you a friendly person?**
   ❏ Yes, I'm very **outgoing**. I have a lot of friends, and I like to meet new people. (*James, 18*)
   ❏ I'm a nice guy, but I'm not very **talkative**. I have two or three good friends. I talk to them a lot. But with other people, I'm shy. (*Carlos, 23*)

Carlos is shy.

2. Are you interested in fashion?

❑ I usually wear old jeans and T-shirts. I don't care about people's clothes. I'm more interested in someone's **personality**. (*Hassan, 22*)

❑ Clothes are important. I like to dress well. People say I'm very **fashionable**. (*Matt, 21*)

Rob is tall.

3. How tall are you?

❑ I'm tall—about 192 centimeters. I play basketball for City University. (*Rob, 20*)

❑ I have two brothers. They are both very tall—about 198 centimeters! But I'm only **average** height—about 179 centimeters. (*David, 19*)

4. Are you a neat person?

❑ I don't have time to clean. I go to school and I also have a part-time job. I'm always busy! (*Kate, 21*)

❑ I can't study in a **messy** room. I'm very busy, but I clean my room every day. (*Amanda, 18*)

5. Are you a serious or funny person?

❑ I study a lot, so people think I'm a very **serious** person. But I also like to have fun. (*Sarah, 21*)

❑ I love to laugh and tell jokes. (*Emma, 24*)

Sarah is serious.

6. What is your best subject in school?

❑ I'm good at math. It's my favorite subject. For some people, math is hard. For me, it is easy. (*Khalid, 18*)

❑ My best subjects are English and French. I also speak Spanish! (*Pablo, 17*)

COMPREHENSION CHECK

A. Read the statements. Write *T* (true) or *F* (false). Then correct each false statement to make it true.

____ 1. James likes to meet new people.

____ 2. Carlos is very talkative.

____ 3. Hassan is fashionable.

____ 4. David is tall.

____ 5. Kate is a very neat person.

____ 6. Amanda's room is messy.

____ 7. Sarah studies very hard.

____ 8. Emma is a very serious person.

____ 9. Math is easy for Khalid.

____ 10. Pablo is good at English.

B. Work with a partner. Choose three questions from the article. Ask and answer your questions. Explain your answers.

A: Are you a friendly person?
B: Yes, I'm very talkative.

Building Vocabulary | **Descriptive adjectives**

We use **adjectives** to describe people.

Adjectives for appearance	Adjectives for personality
Height: tall, short, average height	kind, friendly, helpful, nice
Weight: heavy, thin, average weight	generous
Hair: blond, brown, red, black	shy, quiet
Appearance: handsome,	smart, intelligent
good-looking, pretty, cute	funny, serious

A. Complete the sentences. Circle the correct answer.

generous

helpful

1. She's (tall / thin / kind) because she doesn't eat a lot.

2. He is a good-looking man. He is very (handsome / serious / quiet).

3. I laughed because he is a (cute / friendly / funny) guy.

4. Hassan doesn't talk much. He is (short / helpful / shy).

5. Sun-Hee is good basketball player because she is (generous / tall / blond).

6. Thank you very much. You are very (helpful / quiet / heavy).

7. This class is easy for her. She is (funny / smart / pretty).

8. Khalid shares money with other people. He is (generous / serious / handsome).

B. Match the words with their opposites.

1. outgoing ____   a. neat

2. tall ____   b. serious

3. messy ____   c. shy

4. heavy ____   d. talkative

5. funny ____   e. short

6. quiet ____   f. thin

C. What other words describe people? Write them in the chart. Then write five sentences using the words.

Words to describe appearance	Words to describe personality

1. _____

2. _____

3. _____

4. _____

5. _____

Reading Skill	Identifying topics and main ideas	

Every paragraph has a **topic** and a **main idea**.

1. **The topic** Usually, you can say the topic in one or two words. To identify the topic, ask this question: *What is this paragraph about?*

   In this paragraph, the topic is "**my sister.**" The topic <u>repeats</u> in the paragraph.

   > <u>My sister</u>, Megumi, is very popular. Everyone likes her. Why? For one thing, <u>she</u> is very outgoing. <u>She</u> laughs a lot, and <u>she</u> tells jokes. <u>She</u> makes people happy. For these reasons, <u>my sister</u> has a lot of friends.

2. **The main idea** Usually, you can say the main idea in a short sentence. To identify the main idea, ask this question: *What is the most important idea in this paragraph?*

   In the paragraph above, the main idea is "**My sister, Megumi, is very popular.**" The other sentences in the paragraph explain this idea.

Read the article. Then answer the questions below. Circle _a_ or _b_.

Cristiano Ronaldo

1   Cristiano Ronaldo is a famous soccer player. He is from Portugal. He plays for a soccer team in Spain. The team is called Real Madrid.

2   Ronaldo is good at soccer. In his free time, he is also interested in business. He owns two clothing stores in Portugal. One store is in Lisbon and one is in Madeira.

3   Each year, his team pays him $15 million. Companies also pay him to wear their clothes and shoes. Cristiano Ronaldo is a rich man.

4   Ronaldo is also very generous. He uses his money to help people around the world. Sometimes he gives his money to people after a flood or an earthquake. He is a nice guy!

1. What is the topic of the reading? _____

2. What is the main idea of paragraph 1?
   a. Ronaldo is a famous soccer player.
   b. His team is called Real Madrid.

3. What is the main idea of paragraph 2?
   a. One store is in Lisbon.
   b. Ronaldo is interested in business.

4. What is the main idea of paragraph 3?
   a. Companies pay Ronaldo to wear their clothes.
   b. Ronaldo is a rich man.

5. What is the main idea of paragraph 4?
   a. Ronaldo is a serious person.
   b. He gives his money to people.

WHAT DO YOU THINK?

A. Do this magazine survey.

Tip Critical Thinking

In this activity, you **list** words to describe yourself and your partner. Listing is a good way to remember information such as new vocabulary.

Who are you?

Which words describe you?
Check (✓) your answers.

☐ tall	☐ serious	☐ quiet
☐ short	☐ nice	☐ outgoing
☐ handsome	☐ smart	☐ funny
☐ thin	☐ shy	☐ helpful
☐ pretty	☐ friendly	☐ neat
☐ fashionable	☐ talkative	☐ messy

B. Complete these tasks with a partner.

1. Ask your partner about their answers in Activity A. Take turns.

    A: Are you tall?
    B: Yes, I am.
    B: Are you outgoing?
    A: No, I'm not.

2. Write three words to describe both you and your partner.

    _____ _____ _____

3. Ask your partner, "What are you interested in? What are you good at?"
    Write your partner's answers.

    My partner is good at . . .
    My partner is interested in . . .

    _____
    _____
    _____

Present of be

Use the verb *be* to identify and describe people and things.

 Tip for Success

Statements with *be* can be followed by nouns (*a student*), adjectives (*tall*), or prepositional phrases (*from Portugal*).

Affirmative and negative statements				Contractions			
subject	*be*	(not)		subject + *be*	(not)	subject	*be + not*
I	am		a student.	I'm			
You				You're		You	
We	are		tall.	We're		We	aren't
They		(not)		They're	(not)	They	
He				He's		He	
She	is		from Portugal.	She's		She	isn't
It				It's		It	

- A **contraction** makes two words into one word. It has an apostrophe (').
- There are two negative contractions for *are not* and *is not*.

    are not = 're not = aren't   is not = 's not = isn't

Information questions			Answers
wh- word	*be*	subject	
Who	**is**	Toshi's friend?	Sam **is** Toshi's friend.
What	**are**	his interests?	His interests **are** soccer and music.
Where	**are**	you from?	I **am** from Japan.

- In questions, the verb *be* comes before the subject.
- A question ends with a question mark (?).

Simple present

The simple present describes habits, facts, or feelings.

> Sun-Hee **eats** breakfast every morning.
> Matt **goes** to Brown University.
> Sarah **feels** happy today.

Affirmative statements

subject	verb	
I - You - We - They	**come**	from Australia.
He - She - It	**comes**	

Use the base verb + -s or -es after *he*, *she*, and *it*.

Add -*s* after most verbs	ge**ts**, listen**s**, like**s**, play**s**
Add -*es* after -*ch*, -*sh* or -*o*.	do**es**, go**es**, wash**es**, watch**es**
If the verb ends in a consonant + -*y*, change the *y* to *i* and add -*es*.	cr**ies**, fl**ies**, stud**ies**, tr**ies**
Irregular third-person form	have → **has**

Isabel

A. Complete the paragraph with *am*, *is*, or *are*.

My name ___is___ Isabel. I ___2___ from
Canada. I ___3___ tall and my hair ___4___
very long. Right now, I ___5___ a student in Mexico. I
___6___ interested in science. My school ___7___
for international students. The students ___8___ from all
over the world. I ___9___ shy, but it ___10___ easy
to make friends at my school. My classmates ___11___ very
friendly. Sometimes they ___12___ serious, too.

B. Complete the sentences. Use the correct positive or negative form of *be*. Use contractions.

1. John _____*isn't*_____ heavy. He weighs only 120 pounds (54 kilos).

2. You talk a lot. You _____ quiet.

3. I'm not Canadian. I _____ from Kuwait.

4. His height is six feet, four inches (183 cm). He _____ tall.

5. I _____ shy. I am outgoing.

6. Sarah cleans her room every morning. She _____
   a neat person.

7. They _____ good at basketball because they're very short.

8. She _____ a student. She's a teacher.

C. Complete the sentences. Use the correct form of the verbs. (You will not use all the verbs.)

like	enjoy	watch	go
have	take	wash	listen
study	get	make	

1. They _____ TV every night at 8:00.

2. Matt _____ to school every day.

3. Rob _____ his car every weekend. It's a very clean car!

4. Mika _____ to music on the subway.

Mika

5. We _____ a trip every summer.

6. I _____ brown hair.

7. He _____ in the library in the afternoons.

8. Emma _____ good grades in school.

 Tip for Success

A question ends with a question mark (?).

D. Put the words in the correct order to make questions. Then answer the questions.

1. who / teacher / your / is _____

   _____

2. interests / what / your / are _____

   _____

3. you / are / what / at / good _____

   _____

4. are / you / where / from _____

   _____

5. your / when / is / birthday _____

   _____

Unit Assignment   Write sentences to describe yourself

In this assignment, you write sentences to describe your personality, appearance, and interests. Think about the Unit Question, "What kind of person are you?" and use the Self-Assessment checklist on page 17.

A. BRAINSTORM Read the information about Tom on page 16. Rewrite each sentence in your notebook. Make it true for you. Change the words or use *not*.

I am from China. I am not from England.

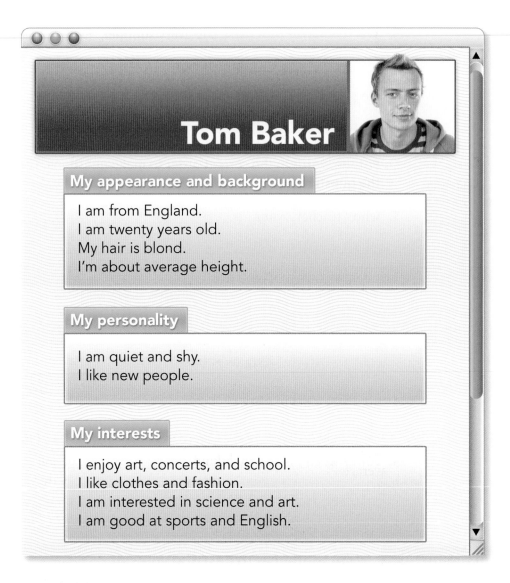

Tom Baker

My appearance and background

I am from England.
I am twenty years old.
My hair is blond.
I'm about average height.

My personality

I am quiet and shy.
I like new people.

My interests

I enjoy art, concerts, and school.
I like clothes and fashion.
I am interested in science and art.
I am good at sports and English.

Tip for Success

Before you write, ask yourself questions. Why are you writing? Who will read your writing? Think about the answers when you write.

B. **WRITE** Answer these questions about yourself. Write two sentences for each question in your notebook. Then share your ideas with a partner.

1. What do you look like?

2. What are you like? Describe your personality.

3. What are you interested in?

4. What are you good at?

C. **REVISE** Work with a partner. Take turns reading your sentences.

1. Ask your partner questions about his or her sentences.

2. Help your partner brainstorm two new sentences.

D. EDIT Review your sentences and complete the Self-Assessment checklist. Make any final changes. Be prepared to hand in your work or discuss it in class.

SELF-ASSESSMENT		
Yes	**No**	
☐	☐	Does every sentence have a subject and a verb?
☐	☐	Do you use the correct verb forms?
☐	☐	Do you use descriptive adjectives?
☐	☐	Do all adjectives come before a noun or after the verb *be*?

Track Your Success

Circle the words you learned in this unit.

Noun
personality 🔑

Verb
describe 🔑

Adjectives
average 🔑
blond
cute
fashionable 🔑
friendly 🔑
funny 🔑
generous 🔑

good-looking
handsome
heavy 🔑
helpful 🔑
intelligent 🔑 AWL
kind 🔑
messy 🔑
nice 🔑
outgoing
pretty 🔑
quiet 🔑

serious 🔑
short 🔑
shy 🔑
smart
talkative
tall 🔑
thin 🔑

Phrases
be good at
be interested in

🔑 Oxford 2000 keywords
AWL Academic Word List
For more information on the Oxford 2000 keywords and the AWL, see page xi.

Check (✓) the skills you learned. If you need more work on a skill, refer to the page(s) in parentheses.

READING	○	I can identify topics and main ideas. (p. 9)
VOCABULARY	○	I can use descriptive adjectives. (p. 7)
GRAMMAR	○	I can use the present of *be* and simple present affirmative statements. (p. 12)
LEARNING OUTCOME	○	I can write sentences to describe my personality, appearance and interests. (p. 15)

UNIT 2

Friendship

READING	●	identifying topics and main ideas
VOCABULARY	●	word families
GRAMMAR	●	simple present
WRITING	●	editing for capitalization and punctuation

Unit QUESTION

Who are your friends?

PREVIEW THE UNIT

A Different friends have different personalities. Write notes about one friend in the chart below. Then describe your friend to a partner.

My friend's name is _____.

Appearance	Personality	Interests

B Look at the picture. What does the number show?

C Discuss the Unit Question above with your classmates.

Listen to *The Q Classroom*, Track 4, to hear other answers.

READING | Different Kinds of Friends

VOCABULARY

A. Here are some words from the Reading. Read the sentences. Then write each bold word next to the correct definition.

1. Here's my **advice**: Buy the blue jacket, not the black one. Blue looks nice on you.

2. Lee: The bus is late!
   Tom: Try to be **patient.** It's coming soon.

3. My older brother is very **thoughtful**. He is very nice to other people.

4. My teachers **encourage** me to work hard. They say I am a good student.

5. David is very **honest**. He never tells lies.

6. The boys' appearances are **similar.** They look like brothers, but they aren't.

7. Mika: This is a good book. What do you think?
   James: I **agree**. It's a very good book.

8. We always **fight** about money. John wants to spend it and I want to save it.

a. _____advice_____ (*noun*) a helpful opinion or suggestion

b. _____ (*adjective*) almost the same

c. _____ (*verb*) to argue

d. _____ (*adjective*) truthful

e. _____ (*verb*) to have the same opinion

f. _____ (*adjective*) not in a hurry; can stay calm and not get angry

g. _____ (*verb*) to tell someone, "You can do it!"

h. _____ (*adjective*) kind and helpful to others

B. Complete the sentences. Use names of your friends and family members. Then read and explain your sentences to a partner.

1. My friend _____ is very thoughtful.

2. I usually agree with _____.

3. I sometimes fight with _____.

4. _____ always gives me good advice.

5. _____ and I have similar interests.

6. _____ is a very honest person.

7. _____ is very patient.

8. _____ encourages me in my school work.

for Success

Photographs and art can help you understand an article. When you preview an article, look carefully at the photographs and art.

PREVIEW THE READING

This article is about different kinds of friends. Work with a partner. Look at the five pictures and the words in bold. Can you say one thing about each picture?

The Listener is a thoughtful friend.

 Track 5   **Read the article.**

Different Kinds of Friends

1   Friends are important for our happiness and our health. There are many different kinds of friends. First, everyone has acquaintances. An acquaintance is a classmate, a neighbor, a co-worker, or a teammate. You say hello to an acquaintance. You sometimes talk a little. But you don't talk about your problems with an acquaintance. Second, you have good friends. A good friend knows you well and understands you. You like to do things together, and you have a good time. Finally, you have one or two best friends. A best friend knows you very well. A best friend listens to your problems and gives **advice**.

2   Every person needs a variety[1] of friends. Different friends help us in different ways. Do you have these kinds of friends?

[1] **variety:** different kinds of things

The Listener

3   A good listener is **patient** and **thoughtful**. This friend understands you well. A listener doesn't talk a lot and doesn't give a lot of advice.

The Listener

The Cheerleader

4   A cheerleader **encourages** you and has a positive attitude[2]. This friend is very talkative and outgoing. A cheerleader always says, "You are fantastic."

The Cheerleader

The Wise Friend

5   A wise friend is **honest** with you. Sometimes a wise friend gives you advice, and you don't like it. But usually, your wise friend is right.

The Wise Friend

The Twin

6   You and your twin are the same in almost every way. You like **similar** things. You always have a lot to talk about. You and your twin **agree** about everything. You don't **fight** with your twin.

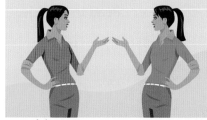
The Twin

The Opposite Friend

7   You are different from this person in many ways, but you are friends. Maybe you don't have the same interests. Maybe you aren't the same age. But you enjoy your friendship.

The Opposite Friend

8   Our friends help us in many different ways. It's good to have different kinds of friends, from acquaintances to best friends.

---

[2] **positive attitude:** an encouraging way of acting

Remember: The topic answers the question, "What is the reading about?" The **topic** is one or two words. The **main idea** of the reading is the most important idea. The main idea is a sentence. Review the Reading Skill box in Unit 1, page 9.

COMPREHENSION CHECK

A. Answer the questions. Circle the letter of the best answer.

1. What is the topic of this article?
    a. acquaintances
    b. appearance
    c. friends
    d. personalities

2. What is the main idea of the article?
    a. Sometimes it's hard to make friends.
    b. It's good to have friends.
    c. A wise friend gives good advice.
    d. There are several different kinds of friends.

3. What are the three kinds of friends in paragraph 1?
    a. acquaintances, good friends, and best friends
    b. classmates, neighbors, and co-workers
    c. a good friend and two best friends
    d. the listener, the wise friend, and the twin

4. What is <u>not</u> in this article?
    a. ways to make new friends
    b. friends that listen well
    c. best friends
    d. friends that are different from you

B. Read the sentences. Write the kind of friend.

the cheerleader	the listener	the opposite friend
the twin	the wise friend	

1. "You and I like the same clothing styles. We have similar haircuts. We like the same kinds of movies." _____ the twin _____

2. "I think you're very smart. You will get a good grade on the test!"

   _____

3. "Why are you so unhappy? Tell me about your problem."

   _____

4. "Think very carefully about your future plans. Plan your school work and your career." _____

5. "I am 20 years older than you. We are different in many ways, but we both love photography." _____

Building Vocabulary | Word families

Word families are groups of similar words. Word families include nouns, verbs, and adjectives. When you learn one word in the family, it is easy to learn other words in the family.

Noun	Verb	Adjective
help	help	helpful
friend		friendly
encouragement	encourage	encouraging

When you learn a new word, learn the **part of speech**. Is it a noun, adjective, or verb?

- Do you need some **help**? (noun)
- I can **help** you tomorrow. (verb)
- My best friend is very **helpful**. (adjective)

A. Label the underlined words. Write _n_ for noun, _v_ for verb, and _adj_ for adjective. Then circle the words that are new for you.

My brother is helpful.

           adj   adj
1. Mika is a <u>kind</u> person. She is very <u>friendly</u>.

2. My brother <u>helps</u> me with my homework. He's <u>helpful</u>.

3. Carlos is very <u>honest</u>. He always <u>tells</u> the truth.

4. I don't need any <u>encouragement</u> to study hard. I want to do well.

5. Her <u>advice</u> to me is clear—practice an hour a day.

6. Sarah <u>wears</u> beautiful <u>clothes</u>. She is very <u>fashionable</u>.

7. My uncle <u>thinks</u> about other people's feelings. He is very <u>thoughtful</u>.

8. My grandfather gives me <u>money</u> for books. He's a <u>generous</u> person.

9. I <u>talk</u> on the phone a lot. I'm a very <u>talkative</u> person.

10. My friends and I <u>have</u> <u>fun</u> at the mall.

Tip Critical Thinking

In activity B, you **classify** words by the part of speech. Classifying information helps you see patterns so you can understand information better. For example, nouns can end in -ness: *kindness, happiness, helpfulness*

B. Complete the chart. Look back at Activity A. (An X means that a word doesn't exist or that you don't need to know it.)

	Noun	Verb	Adjective
1.	friend	X	friendly
2.		X	funny
3.	kindness	X	
4.	happiness	X	
5.	helpfulness		
6.		encourage	encouraging
7.	thought	think	
8.	honesty	X	
9.	fashion	X	
10.	X		talkative

C. Complete the sentences. Use words from Activity B.

1. The children have new bicycles. The children are very

   _____.

2. My neighbor is not _____. She doesn't say hello.

3. I usually _____ my younger brother with his homework.

4. I don't speak very much English. I'm not _____ in

   English class.

5. Emma likes clothes and shoes. She likes _____.

6. This is a good dictionary. It's very _____ for students.

7. We have a very _____ baseball coach. She thinks we

   are great.

8. _____ is very important in business. This store has

   honest employees.

Q WHAT DO YOU THINK?

A. What kinds of friends do you have? Write sentences about four friends. Use ideas from the Reading.

Liz is a wise friend. She gives me advice about my job.

1. _____

2. _____

3. _____

4. _____

B. Describe your friends to a partner.

Liz is a wise friend. She lives in my apartment building. I talk with her about my job. She gives me advice.

The simple present describes habits, facts, or feelings

Affirmative statements

subject	verb	
I - You - We - They	**talk**	about school.
He - She	**talks**	about work.

- Use the base verb + -s or -es after *he*, *she*, and *it*.

Negative statements

subject	do/does + not	verb	
I - You - We - They	**do not** **don't**	**talk**	about school.
He - She	**does not** **doesn't**		about work.

- Use *do* with *I*, *we*, *you*, and *they*.
- Use *does* with *he*, *she*, and *it*.

Yes/No questions

do/does	subject	verb	
Do	you	**study**	hard?
Does	she	**have**	many friends?

Short answers

yes	no
Yes, I **do**.	No, I **don't**.
Yes, she **does**.	No, she **doesn't**.

Information questions

wh- word	do/does	subject	verb	
What	**do**	you	**talk**	about?
Where	**does**	he	**live?**	
When	**does**	she	**call**	you?

Answers

We **talk** about school.
He **lives** in Oman.
She **calls** me after dinner.

A. Write questions with *Do* or *Does*. Answer the questions. Then ask and answer the questions with a partner.

1. you and your friends / study together

   Do you and your friends study together? No, we don't.

2. you / send text messages to your friends

   _____

3. you and your friends / use cell phones a lot

   _____

4. your best friend / have an outgoing personality

   _____

5. your classmates / encourage you

   _____

6. your teacher / give you advice about college

   _____

B. Read about Dan. There are six mistakes in the paragraph. Correct the mistakes.

>   *have*
> Do you ~~has~~ a busy social life? Many people are always busy, but I'm not. I have a quiet social life. I have a lot of acquaintances at school. I likes my classmates. We has a good time in class. We have lunch together in the cafeteria. I have three good friends. We doesn't see each other very often. My friends and I are very busy at school. I also have a best friend. He live in Davis, about one hour from my town. I visit him about once a month. He play soccer and I do, too.

Dan

C. Write questions. Then answer the questions.

1. How many acquaintances / Dan / have ?

   How many acquaintances does Dan have?

   He has a lot of acquaintances.

2. Where / Dan and his classmates / eat lunch ?

   _____

   _____

3. Where / Dan's best friend / live ?

   _____

   _____

4. How often / Dan / visit / his best friend ?

   _____

   _____

5. What sport / Dan / play ?

   _____

   _____

Writing Skill | **Editing for capitalization and punctuation** web⁺

After you write, edit for correct capitalization and punctuation.

Capitalization Rules

1. Capitalize the first word in a statement or a question.

   Friendships are important to me.
   Does your friend live near you?

2. Capitalize proper nouns: the names of people, places, or things.

   My last name is Wong. I'm from Taiwan. I work at City Computers.

3. Capitalize the days of the week and the months of the year.

   Classes start on Monday, October 12.

A. Correct the capitalization mistakes. Add punctuation.

a large family

1. do you have a large family

2. my brother's birthday is february 3

3. the movie is at 5 p.m. on saturday

4. my roommate is from italy

5. my childhood friend lives in caracas, venezuela

6. don't fight with your brother

7. do you study in the library or at home

8. my cousin goes to hong kong university

9. tomas and anna both speak spanish

10. i work at super shoes

B. Read the paragraph. Seventeen words need capitalization. There are seven mistakes in punctuation. Correct the mistakes.

My
~~my~~ brother is my best friend. his name is adam, and he is one year older than I am. we are very different, so he is my opposite friend. he is very quiet and shy he is thoughtful and kind. adam is an excellent student he goes to washington community college. why are we opposites I am very outgoing and talkative sometimes i don't think about other people we have similar interests we both like swimming and sports we do many things together.

In this assignment, you write sentences to describe three friends. Think about the Unit Question, "Who are your friends?" and use the Self-Assessment checklist on page 33.

Tip for Success

Idea maps and charts are graphic organizers. They can help you think of ideas for writing. Use a graphic organizer when you brainstorm.

A. **BRAINSTORM** Follow these steps.

1. In your notebook, draw three idea maps like the one below. Write the name of one of your friends in each of the center circles.

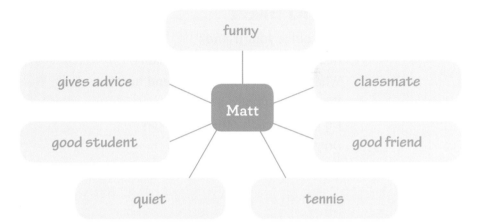

2. Write words about each friend in the outer circles. You can use words from the box below.

Adjectives	Nouns	Verbs
best, curious, fashionable, friendly, funny, good, happy, helpful, honest, kind, outgoing, quiet, serious, silly, similar, talkative, thoughtful	acquaintance, advice, classmate, co-worker, family member, friend, fun, interests, neighbor	agree, be, encourage, enjoy, fight, have, help, listen, live, talk, send (text messages, email), visit

B. **WRITE** In your notebook, write sentences about your friends in Activity A. Write five or more sentences about each friend. Answer some of these questions.

My friend's name is . . .

What's your friend like?

- How old is your friend?
- Describe your friend's personality.
- What interests does your friend have?
- What do you do together?
- Do you see each other every day?
- Do you talk every day?
- Do you always agree about things?

C. **REVISE** Revise your sentences. Follow these steps.

1. Read your sentences. Can you add adjectives to your descriptions?

2. Add another sentence to give more information about one of your friends.

3. Read all of your sentences again. Make any necessary changes.

Tip for Writing

Revising your writing

When you **revise**, you improve the ideas in your writing. You can add adjectives to your descriptions.

> **Original:** My best friend is a student.
> **Revised:** My best friend is an <u>excellent</u> student.

You can add **more information** (details) to your writing.

> **Original:** She is from Florida.
> **Revised:** She is from <u>Miami</u>, Florida.

D. **EDIT** Review your sentences and complete the Self-Assessment checklist. Make any final changes. Be prepared to hand in your work or discuss it in class.

Yes	No	SELF-ASSESSMENT
☐	☐	Does every sentence have a subject and a verb?
☐	☐	Does every sentence start with a capital letter?
☐	☐	Are proper nouns capitalized?
☐	☐	Does every sentence end with a period?
☐	☐	Does every question end with a question mark?

Track Your Success

Circle the words you learned in this unit.

Nouns	Verbs	Adjectives
advice 🔑	agree 🔑	encouraging
encouragement	encourage 🔑	fashionable 🔑
fashion 🔑	fight 🔑	happy 🔑
fun 🔑	help 🔑	honest 🔑
happiness 🔑	talk 🔑	patient 🔑
helpfulness	think 🔑	similar 🔑 AWL
honesty	wise	talkative
ideas 🔑		thoughtful
kindness 🔑		
opposite 🔑		
thought 🔑		

🔑 Oxford 2000 keywords
AWL Academic Word List

Check (✓) the skills you learned. If you need more work on a skill, refer to the page(s) in parentheses.

READING	●	I can identify topics and main ideas. (p. 23)
VOCABULARY	●	I can identify word families. (p. 24)
GRAMMAR	●	I can use the simple present. (p. 27)
WRITING	●	I can edit my writing for capitalization and punctuation. (p. 29)
LEARNING OUTCOME	●	I can write complete sentences about three friends using descriptive adjectives. (p. 31)

LEARNING OUTCOME

Give information about a school using descriptive adjectives and adverbs.

Unit QUESTION

Do students spend too much time in school?

PREVIEW THE UNIT

A Work with a partner. Complete these statements about high school students in your country. Then discuss your ideas with your classmates.

1. High school students spend about _____ hours in school each day.

2. High school students spend about _____ hours on homework each day.

3. High school students spend about _____ months in school each year.

B Look at the photo. Where are the people? What are they doing?

C Discuss the Unit Question above with your classmates.

Listen to *The Q Classroom*, Track 6, to hear other answers.

READING | Comparing Schools in Three Countries

VOCABULARY

A. Here are some words from the Reading. Read the sentences. What do the bold words mean? Circle *a* or *b*.

Tip for Success

The word *school* can refer to any educational institute. The words *college* and *university* often have the same meaning.

1. My classmates study during the **academic** year.
   a. school   b. summer

2. Students **attend** school for seven hours every day.
   a. leave   b. go to

3. I take a one-hour **break** at lunch time.
   a. rest   b. exercise

4. The class **lasts** from 9:00 to 10:00.
   a. begins   b. starts and ends

5. During **study period**, students do homework or read.
   a. special study time   b. discussion time

6. There are three **terms** in the school year: fall, winter, and spring.
   a. time periods   b. months

7. Some students wear **uniforms** to school. Everyone dresses the same.
   a. backpacks   b. special clothing

8. My family usually goes to the beach for summer **vacation**.
   a. holiday time   b. winter time

 **Critical Thinking**

Activity B asks you to **recognize** different parts of speech. When you recognize something, you show that you remember information.

B. What parts of speech are the bold words in Activity A? Write the correct letter above each word: N = *noun*, V = *verb*, A = *adjective.*

C. Complete the sentences with words from Activity A.

1. All students _____ a meeting on Monday mornings.

2. I usually take a short _____ at 10:30. I relax with my friends and have a snack.

3. In Japan, the _____ year starts in April.

4. Each _____ lasts for ten weeks.

5. Players on the team wear _____.

6. The break _____ from 10:00 to 10:30.

PREVIEW THE READING

This magazine article is about the school year in different countries. How long is the school year for high school students in your country?

 Track 7   **Read the article.**

Comparing Schools in Three Countries

1   Do students spend too much time in school? We asked some students to share their ideas about school in their countries.

Marie

2   Marie lives in France. She says, "My school year **lasts** from August to June with four seven-week **terms**. We have one or two weeks of **vacation** after each term, and we have a two-month vacation in the summer.

The school day in France is from 8 a.m. to 4 p.m. with a two-hour lunch **break**. Students don't go to school on Wednesday afternoon, but we **attend** school on Saturday morning. School on Saturday morning isn't very fun!"

Samuel

3   Samuel is from Kenya. He says, "Our **academic** year starts in June. The year has three terms, and each term lasts for

13 weeks. That feels like a long time. We get a one-month break after each term. The school day in Kenya begins at 8 a.m. and ends at 4 p.m. Students pay for school. It's not free like in some other countries. We wear **uniforms** to school each day. All the uniforms are the same color, so they're really boring. We study many subjects, but I think the best part of school is soccer in the afternoon."

Linda

4   Linda lives in the United States. She says, "School begins in late August and ends in June. Then we have a nine-week summer vacation. We attend school about 180 days each year. The school day is about seven hours long. I have six classes and one **study period**.

I like math best. Every night, I do homework for about four hours. I don't have time to relax because my schedule is very busy!"

5   Marie, Samuel, and Linda all think they spend too much time in school. But the amount of time they spend in school is very different.

COMPREHENSION CHECK

A. Read the statements. Write *T* (true) or *F* (false). Then correct each false statement to make it true.

_____ 1. Marie lives in Spain.

_____ 2. There is a one-hour lunch break at school in France.

_____ 3. In France, there are four terms in the school year.

_____ 4. Students in France go to school from Monday to Saturday.

_____ 5. The school year in Kenya begins in January.

_____ 6. Kenyan schools are free.

_____ 7. Students in Kenya wear uniforms.

_____ 8. Students in the United States begin school in October.

_____ 9. In the United States, there is a seven-week summer vacation.

B. Answer these questions.

1. How many weeks of school are there in France? _____

2. How many weeks of school are there in Kenya? _____

3. How many hours of class are there each day in Kenya? _____

4. How many hours of class are there each day in the United States? _____

5. Which country has the shortest school day? _____

6. What information surprises you? _____

Building Vocabulary   Vocabulary log

A **vocabulary log** is a list of new words. It can help you remember words. When you see a new word, write it in your log.

Copy the word in a sentence from the reading.	Then write a new sentence with the word.
New word in context	**My sentence**
1. We have a two-month <u>vacation</u> in the summer.	1. My winter <u>vacation</u> ends in January.
2. We <u>attend</u> school on Saturday morning.	2. Each week I <u>attend</u> a concert in the gym.

 Tip for Success

You can make your vocabulary log in a notebook, on note cards, or on your computer.

A. Start a vocabulary log. Copy these sentences. Write a new sentence with each underlined word.

1. School on Saturday morning isn't <u>fun</u>!

2. Students <u>pay</u> for school.

3. My uniform is <u>boring</u>.

4. I don't have time to <u>relax</u>.

5. I think my <u>schedule</u> is very busy!

6. I think the best <u>part</u> of school is soccer.

7. We <u>attend</u> school on Saturday morning.

8. I do <u>homework</u> for about four hours.

B. Add four more new words from the article to your vocabulary log. Share your sentences with a classmate.

You **scan** a text to find information quickly. When you scan, move your eyes quickly over the passage. Only look for the information you need.

Use these techniques to scan a reading.

1. To find information about a person, place, or country, look for capital letters.

   ☐ **Brian, New** York, **Egypt**

2. To find information about a day or month, look for capital letters.

   ☐ **Monday, October**

3. To find information about dates and times, look for numbers and abbreviations.

   ☐ in **2009,** at **8:30 a.m.,** **five hours**

A. Scan the two paragraphs. Complete these steps.

1. Underline the names of the countries.

2. Circle the number of days in the school year.

3. Put two lines under the times of day and months of the year.

Schools in Germany

1   Eva lives in Germany. She says, "We start school at 7:30 in the morning. That's too early for me! Classes end at 1:30 p.m., so our school day is only six hours. Our school day is pretty short, but our school year is really long. The term begins in September and lasts until July. We take a short vacation in the summer—about six weeks. We study for 200 days each year. But I enjoy school. I study with my good friends, and we learn a lot of interesting things. I think our time in school is about right."

students in Germany

Schools Around the World

2   Around the world, students spend different numbers of days in school. For example, students in France study for 170 days each year, but in Australia and Iran, the school year is 200 days long. The number of hours each day is also different from country to country. The school day in France and Kenya is eight hours long and lasts from 8 a.m. to 4 p.m. But students in France get a two-hour break for lunch, so they only study for six hours a day. Students in Iran start school at 7:30 a.m. and attend class until 3 p.m. Their school day is 7.5 hours long. In Germany, the school day is only six hours long.

students in Kenya

B. Answer the questions.

1. How long is the school year in France? _____

2. How long is the school day in Germany? _____

3. Which country has the shortest school year? _____

4. Which countries begin school at 7:30 a.m.? _____

5. Which country has school for 7.5 hours a day? _____

 WHAT DO YOU THINK?

Write your ideas. Share your answers with the class.

1. Complete the sentence with *too little*, *enough*, or *too much*.

    I think students spend _____ time in school in my country.

2. What is the right amount of time to spend in school? Why?

    _____ hours a day   _____ days a week   _____ months a year

    _____

3. What is the right amount of homework? Why?

    _____ hours a day

    _____

Adjectives

1. Adjectives describe nouns (people, places, or things).

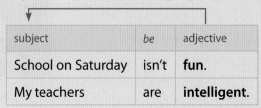

subject	be	adjective
School on Saturday	isn't	**fun.**
My teachers	are	**intelligent.**

- An adjective can come after the verb *be*. It describes the subject.

	adjective	noun
This is a	**new**	school.
I'm taking a	**difficult**	course.

- An adjective can come before a noun. It describes the noun.

2. There are no singular or plural adjectives.

 ✓ Correct: **difficult**
 ✗ Incorrect: difficults

3. Do not use an article (*the*, *a*, or *an*) before an adjective with no noun.

 ✓ Correct: This is a **difficult** test. This is **difficult**.
 ✗ Incorrect: This is a difficult.

Adverbs + adjectives

1. Some adverbs make adjectives stronger.

 Today the weather is **quite** <u>nice</u>. My lunch break is **very** <u>short</u>.
 Pedro's homework is **really** <u>easy</u>. She is **extremely** <u>tired</u>.

2. You can use *really*, *very*, and *extremely* before:

 an adjective alone: This book is **very good**.
 an adjective + a noun: It's a **really nice day**.

A. Circle the adverb and underline the adjective in each sentence.

chemistry

1. I think chemistry is (really) <u>interesting</u>.

2. Soccer is a very easy game.

3. I'm taking an extremely difficult class.

4. This book is quite hard to understand.

5. I like to study in my really comfortable chair.

6. My classmates are very intelligent.

7. I read an extremely boring textbook yesterday.

8. Our lunch break is really short.

9. This homework is very easy.

B. There is one error in each sentence. Find the errors and correct them.

1. My classes are very difficults.

2. This vacation is short very.

3. They were borings classes.

4. She took an easy.

5. My teacher is extremely really.

6. It is a fun homework.

7. The academics year is too long.

8. This lecture is an interesting.

 **for Success**

Learn adjectives in pairs of opposites. For example, *new–old*. Write adjective pairs in your vocabulary log.

C. Complete the sentences with adjectives from the box. (More than one answer is possible.) Then write a new sentence using the opposite adjective.

bad / good	new / old	relaxing / stressful
difficult / easy	important / unimportant	quiet / loud
interesting / boring		

1. I like to study in a _____ quiet _____ place.

   My brother is very loud.

2. My math class is _____.

   _____

3. I like to wear _____ clothes.

   _____

4. That book is really _____.

   _____

5. We have a very _____ teacher.

   _____

6. It is an extremely _____ test.

   _____

7. This English homework is quite _____.

   _____

8. This is a very _____ class.

   _____

Unit Assignment **Give information about a school**

 In this assignment, you give information about a school. Think about the Unit Question, "Do students spend too much time in school?" and use the Self-Assessment checklist on page 46.

A. **BRAINSTORM** What words do we use to talk about schools? Write them in the chart. Then share your ideas with a partner.

Schedule/Time	Classes	Homework
busy	large	difficult

Tip for Success

Use *a.m.* for times from midnight to 11:59 in the morning. Use *p.m.* for times from noon to 11:59 at night.

B. **WRITE** Answer the questions in the survey. Use complete sentences. Use the words from Activity A.

I'm writing about my school. I attend a very large private college.
Our academic year is from September to June.

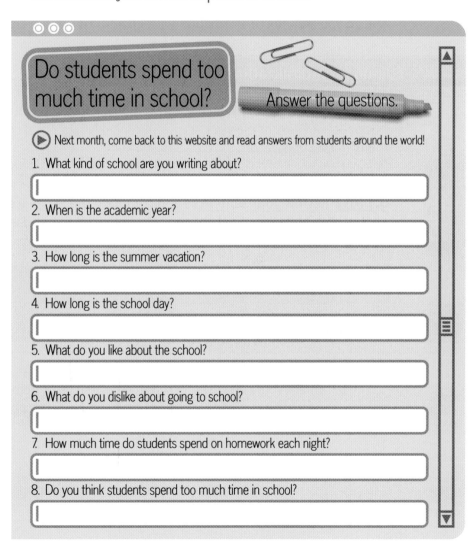

○ ○ ○

Do students spend too much time in school?

Answer the questions.

▶ Next month, come back to this website and read answers from students around the world!

1. What kind of school are you writing about?

2. When is the academic year?

3. How long is the summer vacation?

4. How long is the school day?

5. What do you like about the school?

6. What do you dislike about going to school?

7. How much time do students spend on homework each night?

8. Do you think students spend too much time in school?

ⓣ Tip for Writing

Check your prepositions.
- Use *for* + amount of time (*for 6 hours*).
- Use *at* + specific time (*at 3:00*).
- Use *on* + day of the week (*on Monday*).
- Use *in* + month (*in July*).
- Use *from . . . to* with two times (*from 8:00 to 3:00*; *from January to June*).

C. REVISE Read your sentences to a partner. Discuss the questions below. Then revise and rewrite your sentences.

1. Can you add more specific information by using prepositions and a time or date?

2. Can you add more information with an adjective or adverb + adjective?

| Skill Review | Editing for capitalization and punctuation |

Remember: Start every sentence with a capital letter, and end it with a period. Months and days of the week start with capital letters. Review the Writing Skill box in Unit 2, page 29.

D. EDIT Review your sentences and complete the Self-Assessment checklist. Make any final changes. Be prepared to hand in your work or discuss it in class.

SELF-ASSESSMENT		
Yes	No	
☐	☐	Does every sentence start with a capital letter?
☐	☐	Are months and days of the week capitalized?
☐	☐	Does every sentence end with a period?
☐	☐	Check your adjectives. Do they come after *be* or before a noun?
☐	☐	Check your prepositions. Do you use *for*, *at*, *on*, and *in* correctly?

Track Your Success

Circle the words you learned in this unit.

Nouns
break 🔑
schedule 🔑 AWL
study period
term
uniform 🔑 AWL
vacation 🔑

Verbs
attend
enjoy 🔑
last 🔑
pay 🔑
relax 🔑 AWL

Adjectives
academic 🔑 AWL
boring 🔑
busy 🔑
difficult 🔑
easy 🔑
fun 🔑
important 🔑
interesting 🔑
relaxing AWL
stressful AWL
unimportant

Adverbs
extremely 🔑
quite 🔑
really 🔑
very 🔑

🔑 Oxford 2000 keywords
AWL Academic Word List

Check (✓) the skills you learned. If you need more work on a skill, refer to the page(s) in parentheses.

READING ●	I can scan for names, dates, and times. (p. 40)
VOCABULARY ●	I can use a vocabulary log. (p. 39)
GRAMMAR ●	I can use adjectives and adverbs + adjectives. (p. 42)
WRITING ●	I can edit my writing for capitalization and punctuation. (p. 46)
LEARNING OUTCOME ●	I can give information about a school using descriptive adjectives and adverbs. (p. 44)

READING	●	scanning for information
VOCABULARY	●	using the dictionary
GRAMMAR	●	verbs + gerunds or infinitives
WRITING	●	writing complete sentences

Unit QUESTION

When do we eat special foods?

PREVIEW THE UNIT

A **Answer the questions. Then share your answers with a partner.**

1. What snacks do you like to eat? What is your favorite dinner? What is your favorite dessert?

2. Why do you usually eat? Check (✓) the boxes.

I eat because . . .

☐ I'm hungry.   ☐ it's fun to do with friends.
☐ it's time for a meal.   ☐ I like to be with my family.
☐ I'm bored.

B **Look at the photo. Who are the people? What are they doing?**

C **Discuss the Unit Question above with your classmates.**

🔊 Listen to *The Q Classroom*, Track 8, to hear other answers.

READING | Celebrating the New Year with Food

VOCABULARY

Here are some words from the Reading. Look at the photos and read the sentences. Then write each bold word next to the correct definition.

a. I use **ingredients** from my garden—tomatoes, peppers, and onions. I like **fresh** vegetables, not canned or frozen ones.

b. The New Year is a **special** night for people around the world. Some people **celebrate** New Year's Eve with friends.

c. Cookouts are **popular** for summer holidays. Some **traditional** menus include grilled hamburgers or chicken, potato salad, and fresh watermelon.

d. In Canadian **culture**, Thanksgiving Day is a holiday in October. Families **prepare** a turkey dinner and enjoy relaxing together.

1. _____ (*adjective*) not usual or ordinary

2. _____ (*adjective*) not frozen or in a can

3. _____ (*verb*) to make (a dish or a meal)

4. _____ (*verb*) to do something fun for a holiday

5. _____ (*adjective*) liked or enjoyed by a lot of people

6. _____ (*noun*) the things you use to make a meal

7. _____ (*noun*) habits, ideas, or beliefs of a country

8. _____ (*adjective*) based on a belief or habit that started in the past and continues now

PREVIEW THE READING

This magazine article is about special New Year's food. Look quickly over the article. Check (✓) the true statements about the article.

- ☐ 1. The topic of this article is food in the United States.
- ☐ 2. There is a paragraph about beans.
- ☐ 3. There is a paragraph about different types of meat.
- ☐ 4. The article describes New Year's foods in different countries.
- ☐ 5. The topic of this article is unusual foods.

 Track 9 **Read the article.**

Celebrating the New Year with Food

1 The New Year is a very **special** occasion. We say goodbye to the last year, and we think about the future. We **celebrate** with family members, friends, and neighbors. **Cultures** around the world celebrate the New Year, but everyone celebrates it a little differently. For everyone, New Year's means special food.

Chinese New Year Cake

making Vietnamese rice cake

2 In many parts of the world, rice is the most important **ingredient** in New Year's foods. People **prepare** rice in many different ways—from rice cakes to rice soup. In Korea, parents encourage children to eat all of their rice cake soup for a good year. In Vietnam, people carefully wrap a rice cake in a large, **fresh** green leaf. This makes a perfect square cake. In China, the New Year Cake is a special sweet cake with rice. Every area of China has a different kind of New Year Cake.

3 In other parts of the world, beans are the common ingredients in many New

Year's dishes. Everyone prepares beans in a different way. Italians enjoy eating green lentils, a kind of bean. In Brazil, families like to cook special lentils and rice. Sweet black beans are **popular** in Japan on New Year's. In the southern United States, families like eating a special kind of bean dish called "black-eyed peas."

"black-eyed peas"

4   Some cultures have some unusual traditions for the New Year. In Mexico and other Spanish-speaking countries, at midnight, each person eats 12 grapes in one minute. Each grape is for a month. If a grape is sour, maybe that will be a bad

month in the New Year. For the Persian New Year, the **traditional** table has the seven "S's." There are seven foods. Each food begins with the Persian letter *S*.

the seven "S's"

5   In the United States and Canada, many people like to go to parties on New Year's Eve. At midnight, everyone cheers[1]. On New Year's Day, families enjoy eating special foods from around the world. Because people in the U.S. and Canada are from so many different cultures, there isn't one traditional food that everyone eats. Every family has special foods for the holiday.

[1] **cheers:** shouts loudly because they are happy

COMPREHENSION CHECK

Tip Critical Thinking

In Activity A, you locate an idea in a paragraph. **Locating** means finding the place of the idea. This shows you understand ideas even when the words are different.

A. Write the correct paragraph number next to each main idea.

a. There are many unusual traditions for the New Year. ____

b. Beans are popular in New Year's dishes. ____

c. People in the United States and Canada don't have only one traditional New Year's food. ____

d. People use rice as the main ingredient in many New Year's foods. ____

e. People around the world eat special foods for the New Year. ____

Remember: You scan a text to find information quickly. Only look for the information you need. To find information about a person, place, or country, look for capital letters. You can also scan for a specific word. Review the Reading Skill box in Unit 3, page 40.

B. Read each question. Then scan the Reading on pages 51–52 to find the underlined word. Answer the question.

1. In <u>Vietnam</u>, what do people make with rice? _____

2. What is an unusual custom in <u>Mexico</u>? _____

   _____

3. What are <u>lentils</u>? _____

4. What are the seven "S's"? _____

   _____

5. What do people eat in the <u>southern United States</u>? _____

   _____

6. What is the New Year Cake in <u>China</u>? _____

Building Vocabulary | Using the dictionary

You can build your vocabulary by **using the dictionary**. Look at the entry.

> **fruit** 🔑 /frut/ *noun* [*count, noncount*]
>
> ---
> **ℹ PRONUNCIATION**
> The word **fruit** sounds like **boot**.
>
> ---
> the part of a plant or tree that holds the seeds. Oranges and apples are types of **fruit**: *Would you like a **a piece of fruit**?* • *"Would you like **some** fruit?" "Yes please – I'll have a pear."*

Use the dictionary entry to learn new words. In this definition for *fruit,* you can learn other important words: *plant, tree,* and *seeds.* You learn that oranges, apples, and pears are types of fruit. In addition, many learners' dictionaries have color illustrations to show vocabulary.

All dictionary entries are from the *Oxford Basic American Dictionary for learners of English* © Oxford University Press 2011.

Learn words to
describe food:
*delicious, fresh, bitter,
spicy, salty, sweet,* and
sour. These adjectives
answer the question,
"How does it taste?"

A. Look at these dictionary entries. Answer the questions.

1.

> **dai·ry** /ˈdɛri/ *noun (plural* **dai·ries***)*
>
> ❶ SPELLING
> Be careful! Don't confuse **dairy** and **diary**.
> You spell **dairy** with **AI**.
>
> **1** [*count*] a place where milk is kept, or where
> milk products like butter and cheese are made
> **2** [*noncount*] food made from milk, for example
> cheese or butter: *Don't give her a yogurt – she
> doesn't eat dairy.* • *dairy products*

a. Which definition number is for a place? A food? _____

b. What are three dairy products in the entry? _____

_____

c. Write a sentence with the word *dairy* in your notebook.

2.

> **meal** 🔑 /mil/ *noun* [*count*]
> food that you eat at a certain time of the day:
> *What's your favorite meal of the day?* • *We **had** a
> nice **meal** in that restaurant.*
>
> **Culture**
>
> ■ **Breakfast**, **lunch**, and **dinner** are the usual
> meals of the day.
> ■ We do not usually use "a" with the names
> of meals: *Let's **have lunch** together
> tomorrow.*

a. What are three meals? _____

_____

b. Can you eat a meal in a restaurant? _____

c. Write a sentence with the word *meal* in your notebook.

3.

> **veg·e·ta·ble** 🔑 /ˈvɛdʒtəbl/ *noun* [*count*]
> a plant or part of a plant that we eat: *The
> students grow vegetables such as cabbages,
> beans, and carrots.*

a. What are three types of vegetables in the entry? _____

_____

b. Can you name more vegetables? _____

c. Write a sentence with the word *vegetable* in your notebook.

B. Make a food chart in your vocabulary log. Add the words in the box, and then add more foods. If necessary, use a dictionary. Compare your chart with your partner.

apple	chicken	beef	lobster	milk
onion	potato	fish	cheese	grapes
banana	beans	shrimp		

Fruit	Vegetables	Meat	Seafood	Dairy products
apple				

 WHAT DO YOU THINK?

A. Write your favorite celebration in the chart. It can be a birthday, anniversary, or holiday. Answer the questions.

	My favorite celebration	My partner's favorite celebration
1. When do you usually have this celebration?		
2. What special foods do you eat? Why?		
3. What is your favorite food at this celebration?		

B. Interview your partner and complete the chart.

1. Gerunds and infinitives are usually words for activities.
   - A gerund is a **base verb** + **-ing:** *running, swimming, eating.*
   - An infinitive is **to** + **a base verb:** *to cook, to prepare, to bake.*

2. **Verbs + gerunds** You can use gerunds after some verbs.

subject	verb	gerund
He	**enjoys**	**cooking.**
We	**avoid***	**eating** candy.

3. **Verbs + infinitives** You can use infinitives after some verbs.

subject	verb	infinitive
She	**tries**	**to eat** healthy food.
We	**need**	**to bake** the cake.
They	**want**	**to have** a snack.

4. **Verbs + infinitives <u>or</u> gerunds** You can use gerunds or infinitives after some verbs.

subject	verb	gerund or Infinitive
He	**likes**	**to eat** at home. **eating** at home.
We	**hate**	**to cook.** **cooking.**
They	**love**	**to eat** out at restaurants. **eating** out at restaurants.

*** avoid:** to try not to do something; to stay away from

in a supermarket

A. Complete the sentences. Use verb + gerund or verb + infinitive.

1. Every week, I _____ *need to buy* _____ (need / buy) food at the supermarket.

2. Sam is heavy, so he _____ (avoid / eat) candy.

3. I _____ (try / eat) lunch every day, but sometimes I don't have time.

4. Toshi _____ (hate / cook), but he washes the dishes after dinner.

5. Anna _____ (hate / wash) dishes.

6. My classmates _____ (enjoy / have) coffee together after class.

7. My neighbor _____ (love / watch) cooking programs on TV.

8. My cousin _____ (want / be) a famous cook on TV.

B. Answer the questions. Use verb + infinitive or verb + gerund.

1. What do you like to eat for breakfast?

   _____

2. What foods do you like to prepare?

   _____

3. What vegetable do you hate eating?

   _____

4. What snack do you enjoy eating with your friends?

   _____

5. What foods do you avoid eating?

   _____

Every sentence needs a **subject** and a **verb**. The **subject** is a noun or pronoun. It answers the question "Who or what is the sentence about?" The **verb** is the action. It answers the question "What does the subject do, think, or feel?"

I prepare dinner every day.
subject verb

Usually my dinners are delicious.
subject verb

My friends like to go to cafés.
subject verb

Right now, they are at a café.
subject verb

Always make your subject and verb agree.

✓ Correct: I like oranges. ← Subject and verb agree.
✓ Correct: He likes oranges. ← Subject and verb agree.
✗ Incorrect: He like oranges. ← Subject and verb do not agree.

 for Success

When a sentence has two clauses (parts) joined by *because* or *and*, each clause must have a subject and a verb. *I like* cake because *it is* sweet.

A. Add a subject (*he, she, it,* or *they*) or the verb *be* to each sentence.

1. My brother is a student in a cooking program.

2. Is a very difficult book.

3. There delicious dishes on this menu.

4. Are very good cookies.

5. Is an excellent baker.

6. Kate at the café this afternoon.

7. I rarely eat seafood because it usually very expensive.

8. Carlos likes to eat in restaurants because doesn't like cooking.

B. Correct the incorrect verb in each sentence.

1. Sam ~~go~~ goes to the cafeteria after class.

2. Mary have a new job as a waitress.

3. They loves to eat popcorn at the movie theater.

4. Hassan prepare coffee every morning.

5. I are at the same table as my friends.

6. Isabel don't like baking cakes.

7. We like eating chicken on Saturdays and we usually has steak on Sundays.

8. My family like to have dinner together because we enjoy talking.

C. Write sentences about yourself with the words in parentheses. Change the verb if necessary. Label the subject and verb in each sentence.

1. (enjoy going out) <u> S   V   I enjoy going out for breakfast.   </u>

2. (avoid eating) _____

3. (like to eat) _____

4. (enjoy preparing) _____

5. (like to celebrate) _____

Unit Assignment | **Describe a special meal or celebration**

 In this assignment, you describe a special meal or celebration. Think about the Unit Question, "When do we eat special foods?" and use the Self-Assessment checklist on page 60.

A. **BRAINSTORM** Look at the categories in the idea map below. Then draw an idea map in your notebook. Complete the map with words about a special meal or celebration. Then explain your map to a partner.

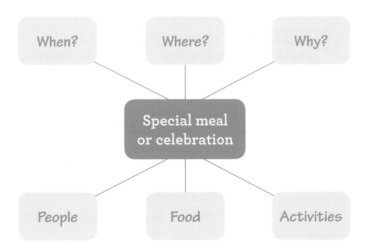

B. **WRITE** Answer these questions about a special meal or celebration. Write a sentence for each question in your notebook.

1. What is the special meal or celebration?

2. When does it happen?

3. What do you need to do before the meal?

4. Do you enjoy preparing the food? Why or why not?

5. Where do you have the meal?

6. Who comes to the celebration?

7. What are the main dishes?

8. Why is the food special?

9. Which food do you love eating?

10. Which food do you avoid eating? Why?

C. **REVISE** Read your sentences to a partner. Discuss your answers. Then revise your writing.

D. **EDIT** Review your sentences and complete the Self-Assessment checklist. Make any final changes. Be prepared to hand in your work or discuss it in class.

SELF-ASSESSMENT		
Yes	No	
☐	☐	Does every sentence have a subject and a verb?
☐	☐	Does every sentence start with a capital letter and end with a period?
☐	☐	Are months and days of the week capitalized?
☐	☐	Do you use infinitives and gerunds correctly?

Track Your Success

Circle the words you learned in this unit.

Nouns
culture 🔑 AWL
dairy
fruit 🔑
ingredient
meal 🔑
meat 🔑
seafood
vegetable 🔑

Verbs
avoid 🔑
enjoy 🔑
celebrate 🔑
need 🔑
prepare 🔑
try 🔑
want 🔑

Adjectives
fresh 🔑
popular 🔑
special 🔑
traditional AWL

🔑 Oxford 2000 keywords
AWL Academic Word List

Check (✓) the skills you learned. If you need more work on a skill, refer to the page(s) in parentheses.

READING ⚪	I can scan for information. (p. 53)
VOCABULARY ⚪	I can use the dictionary to build my vocabulary. (p. 53)
GRAMMAR ⚪	I can use verbs with gerunds and infinitives. (p. 56)
WRITING ⚪	I can write complete sentences. (p. 58)
LEARNING OUTCOME ⚫	I can describe the people, food, and activities at a celebration. (p. 59)

UNIT 5

Fun

READING	● underlining and highlighting
VOCABULARY	● verb + noun collocations
GRAMMAR	● subject and object pronouns
WRITING	● writing complete sentences

Unit QUESTION

How do you have fun?

PREVIEW THE UNIT

A Check (✓) the activities you enjoy. Put an *X* by activities you don't enjoy. Then compare with a partner.

☐ cooking   ☐ watching TV
☐ watching movies   ☐ telling jokes
☐ playing sports   ☐ watching sports
☐ making videos   ☐ going out to eat
☐ going to the beach   ☐ playing cards

B Look at the photo. What are the people doing? Does this look fun to you?

C Discuss the Unit Question above with your classmates.

🔊 Listen to *The Q Classroom*, Track 10, to hear other answers.

63

READING | No Money? Have Fun Anyway!

VOCABULARY

A. Here are some words from the Reading. Read the definitions. Then complete the sentences below.

> **events** (*noun*) important things that happen
>
> **expensive** (*adjective*) costing a lot of money
>
> **guess** (*verb*) to give an answer when you aren't sure
>
> **invite** (*verb*) to ask someone to come to your home, a movie, etc.
>
> **nature** (*noun*) plants and animals
>
> **program** (*noun*) a show on television or radio
>
> **sightseeing** (*noun*) visiting interesting buildings and places as a tourist
>
> **support** (*verb*) to encourage someone

 for Success

Add new words to your vocabulary log. Copy an example sentence with the new word. Then write your own sentence with the new word. Review your vocabulary log often to increase your vocabulary.

1. My friends and I enjoy _____ when we travel to new cities.

2. I like to hike in the mountains because I enjoy _____.

3. Toshi wants to _____ us to come over for dinner.

4. I saw a special person today. Can you _____ her name?

5. There is an interesting science _____ on TV tonight.

6. This newspaper lists the _____ of the weekend.

7. I can't buy that dress. It's too _____.

8. My school's soccer team has a big game tonight. I'll go and _____ them.

B. Work with a partner. Ask and answer the questions.

1. Do you support any sports teams? Which ones?

2. Do you like to spend time in nature? Where do you go?

3. Where do you like to go sightseeing?

4. What kind of events do you enjoy?

5. What is your favorite TV program? Why do you like it?

PREVIEW THE READING

These web posts are about fun things to do without much money. Look quickly at the web posts. What do the people like to do? Write three things.

1. _____

2. _____

3. _____

 Track 11   **Read the article.**

No Money?
Have Fun Anyway!

Question: How do you have fun without much money?
Hi, everyone. I want to have fun, but I don't have much money.
I need ideas. What can you do for free?

James, New York
Posted:
3 days ago

Anna, Miami
Posted:
3 days ago

1. Re: How do you have fun without much money?

James, why don't you go to your school's sporting **events**? I go to games every weekend. I watch soccer, basketball, baseball games, everything! It's fun to spend time with friends and **support** the school. And it's free!

Razi, Dubai
Posted:
2 days ago

2. Re: How do you have fun without much money?

I go window shopping with my friends! We go to **expensive** stores, but we only look—we don't buy anything. So it doesn't cost anything.

Isabel, Santiago
Posted:
12 hours ago

3. Re: How do you have fun without much money?

Our family likes going to the park. We take walks and enjoy **nature** there. Sometimes we have coffee and watch people. We try to **guess** their names and jobs. Try it!

Sun-Hee, Seoul
Posted:
8 hours ago

4. Re: How do you have fun without much money?

I make funny videos with my friends in my apartment. Then we post the videos online and our other friends watch them. It's fun! You can see one here.

Carlos, El Salvador
Posted:
4 hours ago

5. Re: How do you have fun without much money?

Invite some friends to your house and cook together! My friends and I cook together once a month. First, we decide on a meal. Then we shop for the ingredients and prepare the food. We usually cook food from a different country. My favorite was Brazil. It's fun to eat with friends and try new recipes.

6. Re: How do you have fun without much money?

I like to just stay home and watch TV. There are lots of good **programs** and it's free. That's the best way to have fun.

Khalid, Cairo
Posted:
2 hours ago

7. Re: How do you have fun without much money?

Sightseeing is fun, and you don't have to be a tourist. You can take a vacation in your own city. Walk around and enjoy the famous places. I usually bring a video camera and make my own movies!

Rob, London
Posted:
2 hours ago

8. Re: How do you have fun without much money?

Thanks, everyone, for all of your ideas. I'll try some of them!

James, New York
Posted:
1 hour ago

COMPREHENSION CHECK

A. Match the person with the activity.

1. Anna ____   a. go sightseeing

2. Razi ____   b. watch TV

3. Isabel ____   c. make videos

4. Sun-Hee ____   d. go window shopping

5. Carlos ____   e. cook with friends

6. Khalid ____   f. watch people in the park

7. Rob ____   g. watch sports

B. Answer the questions. Find the information from the Reading on pages 65–67. Write complete sentences.

1. Why is it fun to watch a school's sporting events? _____

   _____

2. What are three things to do in the park? _____

   _____

3. Which activity costs some money? _____

   _____

4. Where can you go sightseeing? What are two things to do? _____

   _____

Building Vocabulary **Verb + noun collocations**   web

Collocations are words that we often use together. For example, we use the verb *play* with the noun *soccer*.

   ⌐ **I play soccer.**

We don't use the verbs *do* or *go* with *soccer*.

   ⌐ ✗ Incorrect: I do soccer.
   └ ✗ Incorrect: I go soccer.

Other collocations:

   ⌐ give someone a ride   have an idea
   └ take a trip   make a video

make a video

give someone a ride

68 **UNIT 5** | How do you have fun?

A. In each collocation, circle the verb. Underline the noun.

1. Mika and Emma **are having coffee** together.

2. Let's **make plans** for Saturday night.

3. I **have an idea**! Let's go to the zoo.

4. Toshi **has fun** learning Spanish.

5. Mary **takes a walk** every day.

6. He **makes friends** with new people easily.

7. Are you hungry? **Have a snack**.

8. I am tired. I **am taking a vacation**!

9. **Tell** me **a joke**. I need to hear something funny.

10. On weekends I **play the piano** a lot.

B. Write a sentence using each collocation.

1. (to make plans) _____

2. (to have an idea) _____

3. (to have fun) _____

4. (to take a walk) _____

5. (to have coffee) _____

6. (to make friends) _____

7. (to have a snack) _____

8. (to take a vacation) _____

9. (to tell someone a joke) _____

10. (to play the piano) _____

When you read a text, <u>underline</u> or highlight the important information. This helps you remember it. Do not mark every word on the page. Mark *only* the important information.

Highlight or underline:

- The main idea or topic of a paragraph
- Information such as names, dates, or times

Tip Critical Thinking

Activity A asks you to highlight or underline important information. Underlining helps you **differentiate** between important ideas and extra information.

A. Read the newspaper article. Highlight or underline the important information. Then answer the questions.

COMING EVENTS

1 **Storytelling.** Come listen to Jim Maddox and Mary Weston tell stories for a winter night on Wednesday, December 21, at 7 p.m. at the Davidson Library. Jim and Mary are well-known storytellers. Their stories are all about fun in the winter. Jim and Mary will also show their many photos of birds and animals. Come and enjoy a wonderful evening.

2 **Video contest.** High school students: Do you want to learn to make videos? We can teach you. The best video will win a prize of $250. We will also show the best three videos on our local TV station. For more information, meet at the Town Hall at 2 p.m. on Thursday, December 22. You can borrow a camera from the library. Come, learn, and improve your movies!

1. What is the date of the storytelling event? _____

2. Where will the storytelling event take place? _____

3. How much money is the prize in the video contest? _____

4. What time is the video contest? _____

5. Where can you borrow a camera? _____

B. Look at the Reading on pages 65–67 again. What fun activity does each person like? Underline or highlight the activity.

 ## WHAT DO YOU THINK?

A. Answer the questions.

1. What activities are fun for shy and quiet people?

   _____

   _____

2. What activities are fun for outgoing and talkative people?

   _____

   _____

3. What activities are fun for serious people?

   _____

   _____

B. Compare your answers with the class. What answers are the same? What answers are different? Who do you agree with?

1. Subjects and objects can be nouns.
    *   Subjects come before verbs in statements.
    *   Objects come after verbs or prepositions, like *at*, *in*, and *on*.

subject	verb	object	preposition + object
Kate	likes	the **book**.	
My **brother**	runs	—	in the **park**.

2. Pronouns replace nouns.
    *   You use some pronouns for subjects.
    *   You use some pronouns for objects.

	subject pronoun	object pronoun
singular	**I** enjoy playing video games.	Do you want to play with **me**?
	You are a good cook.	Let me give **you** a new recipe.
	He likes making videos.	Let's give **him** a new video camera.
	She is a very nice person.	I like **her** a lot.
	Where's the ball? **It's** in the car.	Throw **it** to me!
plural	**We** like going to the beach.	Our friends always sit with **us**.
	You always support our team.	We want to give **you** this team photo.
	They play soccer with us.	We always beat **them**.

3. You usually use pronouns *he/him*, *she/her*, *it/it*, *we/us*, and *they/them* after you know the noun.

    Kate likes the book. **She** thinks **it's** very interesting. (Kate = **she**; the book = **it**)

4. A **gerund** (verb + *-ing*) acts like a noun. The pronoun *it* replaces a gerund.

    I like **swimming**. **It's** fun.

    gerund

A. Underline the pronouns. Then circle the noun that each pronoun refers to. Draw an arrow from the pronoun to the noun.

1. (Sarah and Jill) went to the movies. Then <u>they</u> went to a restaurant.

2. Matt likes to play tennis. He enjoys soccer, too.

3. John enjoys cooking. He thinks it is fun.

4. Mika buys many books, but she doesn't always read them.

5. Sarah likes going to the beach, but she can't swim.

6. Ling will kick the ball and Mary will kick it back.

7. After Carlos and Sam watched the game, they made dinner.

8. Hassan and Khalid like playing golf. They are pretty good, too!

9. Mary gave Emma and Tom some videos and they gave her some books.

B. Complete each sentence with the correct subject or object pronoun.

1. <u>Sam</u> and I play tennis together. _____ usually wins.

2. <u>Anna</u> likes to play cards. _____ plays every weekend.

3. I don't like to play <u>golf</u>. I really hate _____.

4. <u>Mary</u> made a video, and I helped _____.

5. <u>Carlos and Isabel</u> come to my house on Wednesdays.

   _____ bring dinner with them.

6. <u>Amanda and Kate</u> play soccer in the park on Saturday mornings.

   Then _____ go out for coffee.

7. <u>John and I</u> are going to take a walk. Maybe you can join

   _____.

8. <u>Matt</u> is playing video games. But _____ needs to take a

   break soon.

9. We like to cook Indian <u>food</u>. _____ tastes very good.

10. My <u>brother</u> enjoys nature. I go to the park with _____

    sometimes.

In this assignment, you write sentences about how you have fun. Think about the Unit Question, "How do you have fun?" and use the Self-Assessment checklist on page 75.

Make your writing more interesting by answering *Wh*-questions—*Who? What? When? Where? Why?*

A. BRAINSTORM Answer the questions in the chart. Make notes, but don't write sentences. Then share your ideas with a partner.

What do you do for fun?	Why is this fun for you?	When do you do this?
1.		
2.		
3.		

Skill Review   Writing complete sentences

Remember to use a subject and a verb in every sentence. Be sure that the subject and the verb are correct. Review the Writing Skill box in Unit 4, page 58.

B. WRITE In your notebook, answer the questions. Use the information from Activity A. Write complete sentences.

1. What is your favorite thing to do for fun?

2. Where do you do this?

3. When do you do this?

4. Who do you do this with?

5. Why is this fun for you?

C. REVISE Read your sentences to a partner. Ask your partner three questions. Answer your partner's questions. Then revise and rewrite your sentences.

D. **EDIT** Review your sentences and complete the Self-Assessment checklist. Make any final changes. Be prepared to hand in your work or discuss it in class.

SELF-ASSESSMENT		
Yes	**No**	
☐	☐	Does every sentence have a subject and a verb?
☐	☐	Are the verb forms correct?
☐	☐	Does every sentence start with a capital letter?
☐	☐	Does every sentence end with a period?
☐	☐	Do you use infinitives and gerunds correctly?

Track Your Success

Circle the words you learned in this unit.

Nouns
event 🔑
nature 🔑
program 🔑
sightseeing

Verbs
guess 🔑
invite 🔑
support 🔑

Adjective
expensive 🔑

Collocations
give (someone) a ride
go window shopping
have a snack
have an idea
have coffee
have fun

make a video
make friends
make plans
play soccer
play the piano
take a trip
take a vacation
take a walk
tell a joke

🔑 Oxford 2000 keywords
AWL Academic Word List

Check (✓) the skills you learned. If you need more work on a skill, refer to the page(s) in parentheses.

READING	●	I can underline and highlight. (p. 70)
VOCABULARY	●	I can use collocations. (p. 68)
GRAMMAR	●	I can use subject and object pronouns. (p. 72)
WRITING	●	I can write complete sentences. (p. 74)
LEARNING OUTCOME	●	I can explain what I do for fun and why I enjoy it. (p. 74)

UNIT 6	Home		
	READING	●	underlining and highlighting
	VOCABULARY	●	word categories
	GRAMMAR	●	prepositions of location
	WRITING	●	writing paragraphs

LEARNING OUTCOME

Write a paragraph describing your favorite room using prepositions.

Unit QUESTION

What is your favorite room?

PREVIEW THE UNIT

A Answer the questions. Then share your answers with a partner.

1. Describe your living room. What color is it? What is in it?

2. What do you like about your home?

3. What do you dislike about your home?

B Look at the photo. What do you see?

C Discuss the Unit Question above with your classmates.

Listen to *The Q Classroom*, Track 12, to hear other answers.

READING 1 | There's No Place Like Home

VOCABULARY

A. Here are some words from Reading 1. Read the sentences. Which explanation is correct? Circle *a* or *b*.

1. Jane: I think someone is smoking.
   Mark: Really? I have a bad cold. I can't **smell** anything.
   a. You smell something with your nose.
   b. You smell something with your eyes.

2. This chair is very **comfortable**. You can sit here and relax.
   a. The chair is expensive.
   b. The chair is nice to sit on.

3. My sisters always come into my bedroom without knocking.
   I have no **privacy**!
   a. I have no space or time away from others.
   b. I have no time to do my homework.

4. I **share** a bedroom with my two brothers.
   a. My brothers and I have our own bedrooms.
   b. My brothers and I have the same bedroom.

5. John is a very **calm** person. He never worries or gets angry about anything.
   a. John is a very relaxed person.
   b. John fights with a lot of people.

6. Mary **collects** postcards. She has 300 postcards from around the world.
   a. She likes postcards and saves them as a hobby.
   b. She sells postcards for a lot of money.

7. There are four windows in the kitchen. When it's sunny, the room is very **bright**.
   a. The kitchen is very dark.
   b. The kitchen is full of light.

8. Hassan likes to **spend time** with his grandparents on Sundays. Usually they have dinner together.
   a. Hassan doesn't have time to see his grandparents on Sundays.
   b. On Sundays, Hassan visits his grandparents for a few hours.

B. Answer the questions.

1. Who do you like to spend time with? _____

2. Where do you go to feel calm? _____

3. Where do you go to have privacy? _____

4. What is something that you share with others? _____

5. Do you collect anything? What? _____

PREVIEW READING 1

This web page is about favorite rooms. Scan the reading to answer these questions.

1. What rooms do people describe?

_____

2. What countries are the people from?

_____

Track 13   **Read the web page.**

There's No Place Like Home

Home and Life Magazine

Last week I asked readers about their favorite rooms in their homes. Wow! I got some great answers and photos! Enjoy reading! And remember, there's no place like home!

I love to cook, so my favorite room is the kitchen. It always **smells** delicious. There is a large window, and you can see the garden from it. Next to the window, there is a small round table. My family and I often have breakfast at that table, but we eat dinner in the dining room.

Makiko, Japan

My favorite room is the family room because I love being with my family. It's a **comfortable** room with a sofa, a TV, bookshelves, and cabinets. There are family photos on the bookshelf. To the left of the TV, there is a fireplace.

Jane, United States

My favorite room is my bedroom. I have a lot of **privacy** because I don't **share** my room with my younger brother. My bedroom is very small, and the colors are boring. My bed is black and my carpet is gray. But I feel **calm** in my room. I **collect** posters, so there are posters of cars, surfers, and animals on the walls.

Ethan, United States

My favorite room is the dining room. On the weekends, we relax and enjoy meals here with my sister and her husband. We sit around a big table. There are several big windows, so the room is **bright** and sunny.

Samira, Lebanon

I love to **spend time** in the basement. Why? Because my friends and I have a lot of fun there! We play games and relax. We can make a lot of noise, too. There's a foosball table, a TV with video games, cards, and board games. There's a big sofa, too.

Hans, Germany

COMPREHENSION CHECK

A. Answer the questions.

1. What does Hans like to do?

   _____

2. Why does Makiko like the kitchen?

   _____

3. Who likes a room for privacy?

   _____

4. Who writes about spending time with family members?

   _____

5. Who writes about a place to spend time with friends?

   _____

B. Circle the correct words to complete the statements.

1. Makiko's family eats (breakfast / dinner) at the table in the kitchen.

2. There's a large (window / table) in Makiko's kitchen.

3. Jane's family room has a (large table / TV).

4. Jane's family room is very (comfortable / messy).

5. Ethan collects (posters / cards) of surfers.

6. It's sunny in Nora's (dining room / kitchen).

7. Hans likes to be (quiet / loud) in the basement.

8. There's a (sofa / bed) in Hans's basement.

Answer the questions. Write complete sentences. Then compare your answers with a partner.

1. In Reading 1, which room do you like best? Why? _____

    _____

2. Which room in Reading 1 is similar to a room in your house? How is it

    similar? Different? _____

    _____

3. Where does your family spend the most time in your home? What do

    you do there? _____

    _____

READING 2 | A Tall Man in a Small Space

VOCABULARY

Here are some words from Reading 2. Read the definitions. Then complete the sentences.

---

design (*verb*) to draw a plan

extra (*adjective*) more than usual

however (*adverb*) but

modern (*adjective*) new, up-to-date; not traditional

neat (*adjective*) well organized; not messy

own (*verb*) to have something

space (*noun*) an open area

view (*noun*) things you can see

---

1. My bedroom has a big closet. I have a lot of _____ for my clothes.

2. Sun-Hee has _____ furniture in her home. She doesn't like old styles and designs.

3. The soup doesn't look very good. _____, it smells delicious.

4. My roommate is very _____. She always puts away her clothes and makes her bed.

5. Rob likes to _____ cars. His drawings are fantastic.

6. We have a(n) _____ bedroom in our house. Our guests stay in it when they visit.

7. My bedroom window has a nice _____ of the street below. I like to watch people walk by.

8. I don't _____ an air conditioner. I plan to buy one next summer.

PREVIEW READING 2

This newspaper article is about one man's very small apartment. Look at the photos on page 84. Answer the questions.

1. What is one good thing about the man's apartment?

   _____

2. What is one bad thing about the man's apartment?

   _____

Skill Review	Underlining and highlighting

Remember: You can underline or highlight important information as you read. Underline one or two important words or phrases in each paragraph. Review the Reading Skill box in Unit 5, page 70.

Track 14   **Read the article.**

A Tall Man in a Small Space

1   Steve Sauer is a very tall man. He's 6 feet 2 inches (187 cm), but he lives in an extremely small apartment. It's only 11 feet by 16 feet (3.35 by 4.88 meters). **However**, this isn't a problem for Sauer. He loves his small apartment. Sauer doesn't like **extra**, unused **space**, and he doesn't **own** many things.

2   Sauer spent seven years building his tiny apartment. He **designed** it, and he also designed and built some of the furniture. The apartment has many open areas. It doesn't have many walls or doors. It has a kitchen with a dining area, a bathroom, two beds, a TV area, and a reading area. In addition, he has space for his two bicycles.

Sauer's kitchen and dining area

Steve Sauer in his apartment

3   When you come in the front door, there is a hall. The bathroom is on the left. Next to the bathroom is the kitchen. In the hall near the kitchen counter, there is a large yellow square on the floor. Lift it up, and you see a beautiful bathtub under the floor.

4   The most interesting parts of the apartment are the beds and the TV area. There is one bed above the bathroom. The other bed is above the closet, at the end of the hall. The TV area is beside the closet. It's a small but relaxing place to watch TV. Above this area, across from the bed, there is a small reading area. It's next to a big window. There is a sunny **view** of the street.

5   Sauer loves his tiny apartment. It is **modern** and **neat**. There is a place for everything important, but there is no space for extra or unnecessary things. In his free time, he loves to design and build things for small spaces. What's his job? He's an interior designer[1] for airplanes!

[1] **interior designer:** a person who designs the inside of a building or other indoor space

COMPREHENSION CHECK

A. Write the correct paragraph number next to each main idea.

___ a. The beds and the TV area are very interesting and unusual.

___ b. Sauer likes to design things for small spaces.

___ c. Sauer is a tall man, but he lives in a tiny apartment.

___ d. In the hallway, there is a bathtub under the floor.

___ e. Sauer designed and built his apartment and some of the furniture.

Tip for Success

Often you can understand something better when you see it. A diagram or a drawing can help you see (or visualize) what you read. This can improve your reading comprehension.

B. Work with a partner. Scan the article again and look at the photos. Label the areas in Sauer's apartment.

bathroom	bed	closet	reading area
bathtub	bed	kitchen	TV area

Level 1

a. _____ _____

TV

b. _closet_____

dining area

c. _____

d. _____

e. _____ door

hall

door

Level 2

window

f. _____ _____

g. _____

h. _____

C. Read the statements. Write *T* (true) or *F* (false). Then correct each false statement to make it true.

____ 1. The apartment is 10 feet by 16 feet.

____ 2. Sauer worked on his apartment for seven years.

____ 3. The bathroom is on the right of the hall.

____ 4. There is a bathtub under the floor of the hall.

____ 5. The TV area is above the reading area.

____ 6. There is a big window in the reading area.

____ 7. The apartment is very modern.

____ 8. Sauer is an airplane mechanic.

Q WHAT DO YOU THINK?

A. Answer the questions. Then discuss your answers with a partner.

1. Do you like Sauer's apartment? Why or why not?

   _____

   _____

2. You can add one room to Sauer's apartment. What room do you want to add? Why?

   _____

   _____

3. Do you know someone with a very small apartment? Describe the apartment.

   _____

   _____

B. Think about both Reading 1 and Reading 2 and discuss the questions.

1. In your home, which room has privacy? Describe the room.

2. In your home, where do you spend time with family or friends? Describe the room.

 **Critical Thinking**

When you **categorize** things, you put them into groups. You can categorize ideas or opinions, types of people, types of entertainment, and so on. Categorizing helps you see similarities between things.

A category is a group of things. You can build your vocabulary by learning words in a category. For example, the category "rooms in a house" includes *living room*, *dining room*, *kitchen*, *bathroom*, and *bedroom*.

A room in a house can also be a category. Put words for furniture and appliances under the name of each room.

living room	bedroom	kitchen
sofa lamp	bed	refrigerator

A. In your vocabulary log, make a chart like the one in the Building Vocabulary box. Then write these words under the correct room. Some words can go in more than one room.

armchair	coffee table	dresser	mirror	sofa
bed	coffeemaker	fan	oven	stove
blender	desk	lamp	refrigerator	table
bookshelf	dishwasher	microwave	rug	toaster

B. With a partner, add more words to your charts. Write them under the correct room.

C. Ask and answer the questions with a partner.

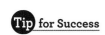 **for Success**

Here are some useful adjectives to describe rooms.
large – small
sunny – dark
colorful – boring
modern – traditional

1. What furniture is in your living room? What adjectives describe your living room?

2. What appliances are in your kitchen? What adjectives describe your kitchen?

3. What furniture is in your bedroom? What adjectives describe your bedroom?

Prepositions of location answer the question "Where?"

The student is sitting **at** his desk.
The ruler is **in** the desk drawer.
The light is **over** / **above** the desk.
The backpack is **under** the table.
The backpack is **on** the floor.
The trashcan is **next to** / **beside** the desk.
The poster is **on** the wall.
The fan is **on the right of** the desk.
The bookcase is **behind** the fan.
The fan is **in front of** the bookshelf.

A. Look at the picture. Write sentences with prepositions of location.

1. lamp / desk _The lamp is on the desk._

2. poster / wall _____

3. bookshelf / bed _____

4. chair / desk _____

5. armchair / window _____

6. photos / bookshelf _____

B. Read this paragraph about the picture on page 88. There are five errors. Find them and correct them.

    I have a typical, small dorm room. It's crowded, but it's comfortable. My desk

is ~~beside~~ _under_ my bed. In my desk, I have my computer and my notebooks. To left

my desk, there is a small bookshelf. I have many books at my bookshelf. There is

an armchair over my desk. I like my room, but next year I want more space for

my clothes. I need a big closet.

| Writing Skill | Writing paragraphs | |

Tip for Success

You can use *there is* and *there are* to describe a room. The verb *be* agrees with the word after it. *There **is** a **closet**. There **are** some **shoes** on the floor.*

A paragraph is a group of sentences about one main idea. A good paragraph has:

1. **A topic sentence** The topic sentence includes the topic (one or two words) and the main idea. The topic sentence is often the first sentence in a paragraph.

    I have a typical, small <u>dorm room.</u>
                               topic

2. **Supporting sentences** The body (middle) of the paragraph has supporting sentences. These sentences give information about the topic sentence.

3. **A concluding sentence** The concluding sentence is at the end of the paragraph. It says the main idea in different words.

    I have a typical, small dorm room. It's crowded, but it's comfortable. My bed is above my desk. There's a big window, so my room is sunny in the morning. I also have a closet for clothes and a small refrigerator for food. My dorm room isn't big, but I like it.

A. Write sentences to complete each paragraph. Use the correct topic sentence and concluding sentence from the box.

Topic Sentences and Concluding Sentences

a. My favorite place is the garage.
b. My family and I spend a lot of time in our family room.
c. We both use the office because it's a quiet space.
d. I like to spend my free time here.
e. My father owns a gardening business, so he has an office in our home.
f. Our new house has a family room.

1. _____

_____

It's a good place to relax and talk. There is
a very comfortable sofa and two armchairs.
We can sit on the sofa and watch TV.
Sometimes I do my homework there.

_____

_____

2. _____

_____

There is a large desk, an office chair, and his
computer. On a small table, there is a printer. He
also has a bookshelf and a file cabinet. At night,
my father works there. When my father is at work
during the day, I study there because it's quiet.

_____

_____

3. _____

_____

I like the garage because I like to work on my car. In the garage, I have my tools and equipment. There are some bright lights, and in the winter, I turn on a small heater. I also have a lot of extra parts for my car. I spend all of my free time working on my car.

_____

_____

B. Complete a description of your classroom. What's in your classroom? What do you do in your classroom? End the paragraph with a concluding sentence.

Our classroom is _____.

Next to the door, there is _____. There are also

_____.

In the front of the room, _____.

The desks are _____. In class, we usually

_____

_____.

In this assignment, you write a paragraph describing your favorite room in your home. Think about the Unit Question, "What is your favorite room?" and use the Self-Assessment checklist on page 93.

A. **BRAINSTORM** Draw a floor plan of your favorite room. Write words to describe it under the floor plan. Then describe your room to a partner.

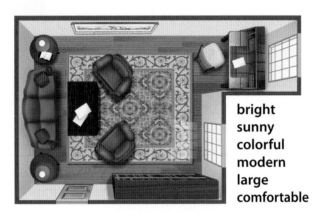

bright
sunny
colorful
modern
large
comfortable

My favorite room in my apartment is my living room. It's a big living room. There's a large sofa and two small tables. . . .

Tip for Success

Always indent the first line in the paragraph. Indent about five spaces. Don't start each new sentence on a new line. Only start a new line for a new paragraph.

B. **WRITE** Write a paragraph about your favorite room in your notebook. Follow these steps.

1. Write a topic sentence. Include a main idea.

2. Write the body of the paragraph. Answer these questions:

   What is in the room? Where are these things?

   What do you like to do in the room?

3. Write a concluding sentence.

C. **REVISE** Follow these steps.

1. Read your room description to a partner.

2. Ask two questions about your partner's room.

3. Revise your writing. Can you add one more supporting sentence about your room?

D. EDIT Review your paragraph and complete the Self-Assessment checklist. Make any final changes. Be prepared to hand in your work or discuss it in class.

SELF-ASSESSMENT		
Yes	**No**	
☐	☐	Check your prepositions. Do you use them correctly?
☐	☐	Do you have a topic sentence?
☐	☐	Do you have supporting sentences?
☐	☐	Do you have a concluding sentence?

Track Your Success

Circle the words you learned in this unit.

Nouns
area 🔑 AWL
armchair
bookshelf
coffee table
dishwasher
dresser
microwave
mirror 🔑
oven 🔑
privacy
refrigerator
sofa
space 🔑

stove 🔑
view 🔑

Verbs
collect 🔑
design 🔑 AWL
own 🔑
share
smell
spend time

Adjectives
bright 🔑
calm 🔑
comfortable 🔑
extra 🔑

modern 🔑
neat 🔑

Adverb
however 🔑

Prepositions
above 🔑
behind 🔑
beside 🔑
in front of
next to
on the right of
over 🔑
under 🔑

🔑 Oxford 2000 keywords
AWL Academic Word List

Check (✓) the skills you learned. If you need more work on a skill, refer to the page(s) in parentheses.

READING ●	I can underline and highlight information. (p. 83)
VOCABULARY ●	I can use categories to learn words. (p. 87)
GRAMMAR ●	I can use prepositions of location. (p. 88)
WRITING ●	I can write a paragraph. (p. 89)
LEARNING OUTCOME ●	I can write a paragraph describing my favorite room using prepositions. (p. 92)

UNIT 7

Weather

READING	•	identifying pronoun references
VOCABULARY	•	using the dictionary: synonyms
GRAMMAR	•	adverbs of frequency
WRITING	•	writing paragraphs

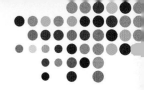

LEARNING OUTCOME

Write a paragraph describing types of weather in answer to a question prompt.

Unit QUESTION

Where is the best and the worst weather?

PREVIEW THE UNIT

A Answer the questions. Use the words in the box or your own ideas. Then compare with a partner.

clear	cold	foggy	rainy	sunny
cloudy	cool	hot	snowy	warm

1. What kind of weather do you like?

   _____

2. What kind of weather do you *not* like?

   _____

B Look at the photo. What do you see? Where do you think this is?

C Discuss the Unit Question above with your classmates.

🔊 Listen to *The Q Classroom*, Track 15, to hear other answers.

READING 1 | Good Weather, Bad Weather

VOCABULARY

A. Here are some words from Reading 1. Read the definitions. Then complete the sentences below.

---

experience (*verb*) if you go to a place, you experience it

freeze (*verb*) become hard because it is so cold

humid (*adjective*) wet (to talk about the air)

pleasant (*adjective*) nice, enjoyable

receive (*verb*) to get something

record (*verb*) to write something down to remember it

terrible (*adjective*) very bad

tourist (*noun*) a person—he or she visits a place on vacation

---

the Canary Islands

1. This city has _____ weather. It's often cold and windy, and it rains a lot.

2. The Canary Islands have beautiful weather. I visited them as a _____.

3. It is very cold here. The lakes and rivers _____ every winter.

4. The April sunshine feels very _____. I like it.

5. Many people travel to Costa Rica to _____ the wonderful weather.

6. Every day, we _____ the temperature in a notebook.

7. In our city, we _____ about 30 inches of rain each year.

8. My hair is curly because the air is very _____.

B. Complete the paragraph with words from Activity A. You will need to add an -s to some words. (You will not use all the words.)

London is the capital city of the United Kingdom. Each year, the city _____ visitors from all over the world. These
1
_____ enjoy visiting the famous places in the city, but
2
they don't usually enjoy the weather. It's _____! It often
3
rains all day. In the summer, the air is very _____. In the
4
winter, sometimes the roads _____
5
because it is so cold. Most tourists don't like to
_____ bad weather. It isn't very
6
_____. But they keep coming to
7
London because it is an interesting city.

PREVIEW READING 1

Scan the reading. What words describe the weather? Underline eight words.

Track 16   **Read the article.**

Good Weather, Bad Weather

What is the weather like in your hometown? Do you think it is bad? Here's our list of the places with the worst weather in the world.

❶ Mount Washington, New Hampshire, United States
The weather is **terrible** on Mount Washington. The wind is always blowing! Sometimes the wind speed is 100 miles per hour (160 kilometers per hour). The weather changes quickly. Each winter, Mount Washington **receives** over five meters of snow. Some **tourists** visit Mount Washington because they want to **experience** the bad weather. They stay at the top of the mountain for one night and pay $500!

❷ Lloró, Colombia In Lloró (pronounced *yo-ro*), the average rainfall in one year is over 40 feet (13 meters). In 1974, the city received 82 feet (25 meters) of rain! It rains about half of the time. Not many people visit this place. If you go to Lloró, take your raincoat and prepare to get wet!

❸ Sahara Desert, North Africa The Sahara Desert is one of the hottest places on earth. The air is extremely warm and dry. Few plants can live there. In the daytime, the temperature is often over 120° Fahrenheit (50° Celsius). Few tourists visit the Sahara and not many people live there. It is too hot!

❹ Antarctica You may be surprised. This cold place is also a desert. That's right: Antarctica is a desert, too, like the Sahara. But it is extremely cold! Once the recorded temperature was minus 130° Fahrenheit (minus 90° Celsius). In the winter, the ocean around Antarctica **freezes** for miles in all directions. Antarctica contains about 90% of the world's ice. Scientists from many countries live and work together in Antarctica. They study nature and **record** the weather.

What makes for good weather?	The World's Best Weather Spots
• The temperature is mild and **pleasant**.	Here's our list of places with the best weather:
• It rains throughout the year, but it doesn't rain a lot.	• Blue Mountains, Australia
• The air is not too **humid** or too dry.	• Cuernavaca, Mexico, "The City That Is Always Spring"
• The weather is about the same all year.	• Tenerife, Canary Islands
	• Honolulu, Hawaii, United States

COMPREHENSION CHECK

A. Match the place with the weather.

1. Mount Washington, U.S.A. ____   a. extreme cold

2. Lloró, Colombia ____   b. strong winds

3. Sahara Desert ____   c. a lot of rain

4. Antarctica ____   d. extreme heat

B. Read the statements. Write *T* (true) or *F* (false). Then correct each false statement to make it true.

____ 1. Tourists pay to stay at the top of Mount Washington.

____ 2. In the winter, Mount Washington receives two meters of snow.

____ 3. In Lloró, it rains half the time.

____ 4. The air in the Sahara Desert is cool and dry.

____ 5. Many plants live in the Sahara Desert.

____ 6. In places with good weather, the air is not too wet or too dry.

____ 7. Tenerife, in the Canary Islands, has terrible weather.

____ 8. Most of the world's ice is in Antarctica.

WHAT DO YOU THINK?

A. Describe the "perfect" weather for you. What place in the world has this kind of weather?

_____

_____

B. Describe the worst kind of weather for you. What place in the world has this kind of weather?

_____

_____

C. Work with a partner. Talk about the places in Activities A and B. Ask three questions about your partner's places and weather.

Pronouns replace nouns. Writers often use a pronoun after they introduce a noun. When you read a pronoun, ask yourself, "What does this pronoun refer to?"

Pedro likes the sun. **He** enjoys sitting in **it** every day in the summer.

Kate and Sarah love the snow. **They** like to throw **it** at each other.

Tip Critical Thinking

In Activity A, you **connect** the meaning between pronouns and nouns. When you read, try to understand the connection between words. This can help you understand the meaning of a text.

A. Read these sentences. What does each bold pronoun refer to? Circle the noun. Draw an arrow from the pronoun to the noun.

1. Some tourists visit Mount Washington just to experience the bad weather. **They** pay $500 to stay at the top of the mountain for only one night!

2. Antarctica is a desert, too. **It** receives only a little rainfall.

3. Scientists from many countries live and work together in Antarctica. **They** study nature and record the weather.

4. Isabel doesn't like to visit her aunt in London because the weather is terrible. **She** prefers pleasant places.

5. Tourists love beautiful weather, and **they** often travel to experience **it**.

6. Every day, Khalid looks at the temperature outside. In fact, **he** often checks **it** three or four times a day!

B. Underline the pronouns in the paragraph. Then circle the noun that each pronoun refers to. Draw an arrow from the pronoun to the noun.

Airplane pilots need to pay attention to the weather forecast[1] because they fly planes in many kinds of weather, and it tells them if flying is safe. A bad storm can slow down airplanes, or it can cause bigger problems! This means the weather forecast is very important. For example, Gary Isenberg is a pilot with Cape Airlines. He sometimes changes his plane's direction because of the weather. Today, pilots have many ways to learn about weather. They can listen to the radio. They can read about it in the newspaper or watch television. And they can get information from the Internet.

[1] **weather forecast:** information to tell you about the weather

READING 2 | Storm Chasers!

VOCABULARY

Here are some words from Reading 2. Read the sentences. Then write each bold word next to the correct definition on page 102.

1. The weather is **severe** on top of Mount Washington.

2. The door is over here. Just **follow** me.

3. My son had to write a **report** about the weather last week.

4. I really like this new blog. I want to write a **comment** on the Web page.

5. Be careful! Skiing during a snowstorm is **dangerous**.

6. Can you **communicate** with people in another language?

7. It is difficult to **concentrate** on your work during a loud storm.

8. Three cars hit each other. It was a bad **accident**.

a. _____ (*noun*) a short statement; it gives your opinion about something

b. _____ (*verb*) to share ideas with someone

c. _____ (*verb*) to pay attention to something

d. _____ (*adjective*) not safe

e. _____ (*verb*) to go after someone or something

f. _____ (*noun*) a written or spoken description of an experience

g. _____ (*adjective*) very bad

h. _____ (*noun*) something bad—it happens by chance

PREVIEW READING 2

This web article describes people who enjoy bad weather. Look at the pictures. Match them to the type of storm.

thunderstorm	tornado	hurricane or typhoon

1. _____   2. _____   3. _____

Which kind of storm do you think is the most dangerous?

_____

Storm Chasers!

1   When a big storm is coming, most people buy extra food, close their windows, and stay home. When a strong hurricane is coming, many people leave their homes. They go to a safe place, far away from the storm.

2   Most people try to stay away from **severe** storms. Not Warren Faidley. Warren is a "storm chaser." Storm chasers love extreme weather. They **follow** thunderstorms, tornadoes, and sometimes hurricanes or typhoons.

Warren Faidley

3   Every day, Warren studies the weather **report.** In fact, he often checks it three or four times a day! When he hears about a storm, he gets into his car and drives, sometimes for many hours. Once, he drove for ten hours because he wanted to see a tornado, but he didn't find one.

4   Warren takes lots of pictures and videos of storms. He really likes to take pictures of lightning. Later he posts them on his storm chaser blog and writes about the storm. Other storm chasers enjoy reading his blog and write back. Warren likes reading their **comments.**

a storm chaser video taping a tornado

5   Storm chasing can be **dangerous.** The weather is one possible danger, but it isn't the worst danger for storm chasers. The worst danger is driving. Storm chasers usually do many things while they drive. They look out the window, check the weather report, make videos of the storm, and **communicate** with other storm chasers. They don't **concentrate** on the road, so they often have **accidents.**

6   If you see a picture or video of a big storm, you can thank Warren Faidley or some of his friends. They aren't afraid of extreme weather. Because of their work, you can watch exciting storms and stay safe at the same time!

COMPREHENSION CHECK

Tip for Success

When you answer multiple choice questions, first find the answers that are clearly incorrect. Then look at the other possible answers. You can choose from two choices instead of four.

A. Circle the answer to complete each statement.

1. When a big storm is coming, most people ____.
   a. open their windows   c. eat more food
   b. stay home   d. get in their cars

2. Storm chasers like to ____.
   a. stay away from storms   c. go outside on nice days
   b. see extreme weather   d. go to safe places in a storm

3. Storm chasers sometimes ____.
   a. stay up all night   c. drive long distances to find storms
   b. watch a lot of television   d. draw pictures of storms

4. Warren likes to share his photos and videos ____.
   a. on the Internet   c. on TV
   b. in the mail   d. in the newspaper

5. The worst danger of storm chasing is ____.
   a. lightning   c. heavy rain
   b. tornadoes   d. car accidents

a storm chaser

B. Write the correct paragraph number next to each detail.

____ a.   The worst danger is driving.

____ b.   Warren really likes to take pictures of lightning.

____ c.   When a strong hurricane is coming, many people leave their homes.

____ d.   Warren once drove for ten hours to see a tornado.

____ e.   Storm chasers follow thunderstorms and tornados.

____ f.   Warren often checks the weather three or four times a day.

 WHAT DO YOU THINK?

A. Discuss the questions as a class.

1.   What do you think of storm chasers? Do you think storm chasing sounds fun?

2.   What kinds of severe weather are common where you live?

3.   Can you think of other kinds of extreme weather?

a blizzard

a sandstorm

B. Think about both Reading 1 and Reading 2 and discuss the questions with a partner.

1.   Why is extreme weather interesting?

2.   Why do storm chasers follow bad weather? Why don't they follow good weather?

3.   What kind of weather is most interesting to you?

Synonyms are words with the same meaning.

Sometimes the dictionary lists synonyms. In this definition, *nice* is a synonym for *good*.

Sometimes you can find a synonym in the dictionary definition. In definition 3, *rain* is a synonym for *shower*.

good¹ /gʊd/ *adjective* (bet·ter, best)
1 done or made very well: *It's a good knife – it cuts very well.* ◆ *The movie was **really good**.*
2 pleasant or enjoyable: *Did you have a good time?* ◆ *The weather was very good.* ⊃ **SYNONYM** **nice**

show·er¹ /ˈʃaʊər/ *noun* [count]
1 a place where you can wash by standing under water that falls from above you: *There's a shower in the bathroom.*
2 the act of washing yourself in a shower: *I **took a shower** after the tennis match.*
3 rain that falls for a short time: *The day will be cloudy, with occasional heavy showers.*

All dictionary entries are from the *Oxford Basic American Dictionary for learners of English* © Oxford University Press 2011.

A. Circle the best synonym for each bold word. Use your dictionary to help you.

1. **clear**   a. mild   (b. cloudless)   c. freezing

2. **muggy**   a. humid   b. snowy   c. dry

3. **sunny**   a. overcast   b. fair   c. chilly

4. **pleasant**   a. nice   b. hot   c. damp

5. **frequently**   a. sometimes   b. rarely   c. often

6. **terrible**   a. noisy   b. awful   c. sad

7. **chilly**   a. cold   b. damp   c. cloudy

8. **lovely**   a. like   b. calm   c. beautiful

B. Use your dictionary to find synonyms for these words.

1. unsafe _____   4. freezing _____

2. severe _____   5. overcast _____

3. damp _____   6. breeze _____

1. Adverbs of frequency answer the question, "How often?"

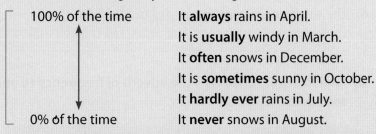

100% of the time   It **always** rains in April.

It is **usually** windy in March.

It **often** snows in December.

It is **sometimes** sunny in October.

It **hardly ever** rains in July.

0% of the time   It **never** snows in August.

Adverbs of frequency come <u>after</u> the verb *be*.	Adverbs of frequency come <u>before</u> other verbs.
It<u>'s</u> **usually** cloudy in Amsterdam.	Carlos **never** <u>wears</u> a raincoat.
It <u>is</u> **always** cold in Antarctica.	They **hardly ever** <u>hear</u> thunder.

2. *Usually* and *sometimes* can also come at the <u>beginning</u> of a sentence.

Usually it's hot in Dubai.

Sometimes they take a vacation in June.

A. Rewrite each sentence. Use the words in parentheses and change the adverb of frequency. More than one answer is often possible.

1. The temperature in this city is <u>usually warm</u>. (freezing)

    The temperature in this city is hardly ever freezing.

2. Storm chasing is <u>hardly ever safe</u>. (dangerous)

    _____

3. The weather is <u>usually dry</u> in the Sahara Desert. (rainy)

    _____

4. Mika <u>never wears</u> light clothing. (heavy clothing)

_____

5. Storm chasers <u>hardly ever walk</u> long distances. (drive)

_____

6. The weather is almost <u>never dry</u> in Lloró. (wet)

_____

B. Take this quiz. Check (✓) the adverb of frequency to answer each question.

The Weather and You

How often . . . ?	ALWAYS	OFTEN	SOMETIMES	HARDLY EVER	NEVER
→ do you carry an umbrella	○	○	○	○	○
→ are you too hot	○	○	○	○	○
→ does the air feel very dry	○	○	○	○	○
→ is it windy	○	○	○	○	○
→ do you wear light clothing	○	○	○	○	○
→ do you check the weather report	○	○	○	○	○
→ are you too cold	○	○	○	○	○
→ do you wear a raincoat	○	○	○	○	○

C. Answer the questions from Activity B in your notebook. Write complete sentences. Use adverbs of frequency.

I *sometimes* carry an umbrella.

In this assignment, you write a paragraph describing types of weather. Think about the Unit Question, "Where is the best and the worst weather?" and use the Self-Assessment checklist on page 110.

A. BRAINSTORM Discuss these questions with a partner. Make notes.

1. Where is the best weather in the world or in your country?

   _____

   _____

2. Where is the worst weather in the world or in your country?

   _____

   _____

3. What is the weather like in these places? Hot? Rainy? Cold? Pleasant?

   _____

   _____

Skill Review	Writing paragraphs

> Remember: A good paragraph contains a topic sentence, supporting sentences, and a concluding sentence. Remember to indent the first line. Review the Writing Skill box in Unit 6, page 89.

B. WRITE Follow the steps below and write a paragraph to answer one of these questions.

- Where is the best weather?
- Where is the worst weather?

1. Write a topic sentence. Include the topic and the main idea of the paragraph.

   _____

   _____

2. Write the body of the paragraph. Use at least one sentence for each idea.

a. What place are you describing? _____

_____

b. Is the weather good or bad? Give an example. _____

_____

c. What do people do in this place? _____

_____

d. What do you like or dislike about the weather there? _____

_____

3. Write a concluding sentence about the weather. Repeat the main idea from the topic sentence. Use different words.

_____

_____

4. Use the sentences you wrote to write a complete paragraph in your notebook.

C. **REVISE** **Share your writing with a partner. Discuss these questions. Then revise and rewrite your paragraph.**

1. What do you like about your partner's writing?

2. What idea or sentence is very clear? Choose one.

3. What sentence could be better? Choose one and say why.

D. **EDIT** **Review your paragraph and complete the Self-Assessment checklist. Make any final changes. Be prepared to hand in your work or discuss it in class.**

SELF-ASSESSMENT		
Yes	**No**	
☐	☐	Does your paragraph have a clear topic sentence?
☐	☐	Does your paragraph include supporting sentences?
☐	☐	Is there a clear conclusion?
☐	☐	Is the first sentence indented?
☐	☐	Check your adverbs of frequency. Are they in the right place?

Track Your Success

Circle the words you learned in this unit.

Nouns	Adjectives	Adverbs
accident 🔑	chilly	always 🔑
breeze	clear 🔑	frequently
comment 🔑 AWL	damp	hardly ever
report 🔑	dangerous 🔑	never 🔑
shower 🔑	freezing	often 🔑
tourist 🔑	humid	sometimes 🔑
Verbs	lovely	usually 🔑
communicate 🔑 AWL	muggy	
concentrate 🔑 AWL	overcast	
experience 🔑	pleasant 🔑	
follow 🔑	severe	
freeze 🔑	sunny	
receive 🔑	terrible 🔑	
record 🔑	unsafe	
	wet 🔑	

🔑 Oxford 2000 keywords
AWL Academic Word List

Check (✓) the skills you learned. If you need more work on a skill, refer to the page(s) in parentheses.

READING ⚫	I can identify pronoun references. (p. 100)
VOCABULARY ⚫	I can use the dictionary to find synonyms. (p. 106)
GRAMMAR ⚫	I can use adverbs of frequency. (p. 107)
WRITING ⚫	I can write paragraphs. (p. 109)
LEARNING OUTCOME ⚫	I can write a paragraph describing types of weather in answer to a question prompt. (p. 109)

UNIT

8

Health

READING ● identifying pronoun references
VOCABULARY ● collocations
GRAMMAR ● modals *can*, *could*, and *should*
WRITING ● supporting your ideas

Unit QUESTION

How can you change an unhealthy habit?

PREVIEW THE UNIT

(A) Look at the habits (regular activities). Which habits are unhealthy? Check (✓) them. Then compare with a partner.

- ☐ sleep four hours every night
- ☐ smoke cigarettes every day
- ☐ eat fresh fruit every day
- ☐ drink a lot of coffee every day
- ☐ eat cookies and cake every day
- ☐ take a walk every morning
- ☐ drink a lot of water every day
- ☐ be very busy all the time
- ☐ have sugary drinks every day

(B) Look at the photo. What unhealthy habits do you see?

(C) Discuss the Unit Question above with your classmates.

🔊 Listen to *The Q Classroom*, Track 18, to hear other answers.

113

READING 1 | When Does a Change Become a Habit?

VOCABULARY

Here are some words from Reading 1. Read the definitions. Then complete the sentences below.

> **behavior** (*noun*) way of acting or doing things
>
> **become** (*verb*) change into; begin to be
>
> **discouraged** (*adjective*) feeling bad or hopeless about something
>
> **expert** (*noun*) a person who knows a lot about something
>
> **give up** (*verb*) stop doing something
>
> **goal** (*noun*) something you really want to do
>
> **lifestyle** (*noun*) the way that people live
>
> **pay attention** (*phrase*) look, listen, or think about carefully

diet

1. Don't let your cough _____ a serious problem. Call your doctor today.

2. Toshi's _____ is to gain five pounds this month.

3. I want to _____ this diet, but my doctor says I need to lose 15 more pounds.

4. Dr. Park is a(n) _____ on food. He teaches food science at the university.

5. My brother eats well and exercises every day. He has a healthy _____.

6. Kate doesn't _____ to her health. She gets sick often.

7. The child's _____ in class is very bad. The teacher will talk with the parents about the problem.

8. I received a bad grade on my math quiz. I'm _____, because I studied hard for the quiz.

This article is about habits. Scan the article to answer these questions.

1. What kinds of habits is this article about? _____

2. How many "stages of change" are there? _____

Track 19   **Read the article.**

When Does a Change Become a Habit?

1   Everyone has a few unhealthy habits. For example, maybe you eat junk food[1], drink a lot of coffee, or smoke. Maybe you get too little sleep, or you never exercise. You know these habits aren't good for you. You should exercise more often, but you don't. Why? Because bad habits are very hard to change.

2   To change a habit, you have to change your **behavior**. It is always difficult at the beginning. But after some time, your new behavior becomes a new habit. **Experts** say that people need 20 to 70 days to change a habit. Some habits (smoking, for example) can take a year to change. According to experts, there are six stages of change.

The Six Stages of Change

1. **Ignoring.** You ignore[2] the problem or don't **pay attention** to it. You don't want to believe that it's an unhealthy habit.

2. **Thinking.** You know your habit is unhealthy, but you don't have a plan to change it.

3. **Deciding.** You decide[3] to change your bad habit. You make a plan to change.

4. **Acting.** You start to change your unhealthy habit.

5. **Making new habits.** After many weeks, your new behavior becomes a new habit.

6. **Going back to old habits.** You go back to your old habit for a day, or a week, or a month. Don't be **discouraged**. This happens to everyone.

---

[1] **junk food:** food that is quick to prepare but is bad for your health
[2] **ignore:** to know something but not do anything about it
[3] **decide:** to think about and choose something

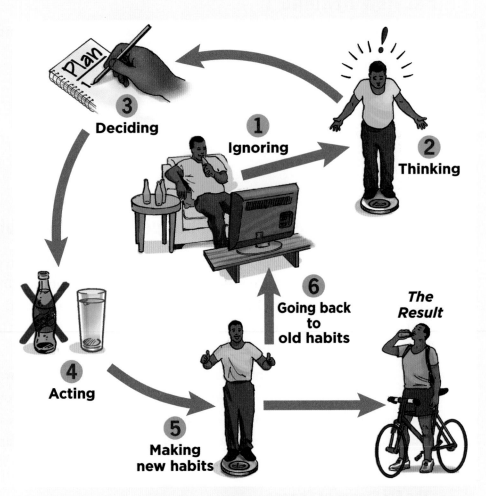

3 People usually want to change their bad habits quickly and easily. Remember, habits take a long time to make, so they take a long time to change. Most people aren't patient. In addition, they don't want to be uncomfortable. For instance, when you start a diet, you feel hungry. If you begin an exercise program, you feel tired or sore. You will probably be uncomfortable when you change a habit, but don't **give up**. Think about your **goal**: a healthy **lifestyle**. With hard work, healthy behaviors can slowly **become** healthy habits.

4 Changing a habit isn't easy. It takes time, and you have to be patient. But the result is a healthier lifestyle and a happier you.

COMPREHENSION CHECK

A. Read the statements. Write *T* (true) or *F* (false). Then correct each false statement to make it true.

____ 1. Most people have only one unhealthy habit.

____ 2. It is unhealthy to eat junk food.

____ 3. Some habits take a day to change.

____ 4. At first it is easy to change your behavior.

____ 5. It's important to have a goal.

____ 6. People hardly ever return to old habits.

B. Read the sentences. What stage of change is each person at?

soda

1. James drinks several sodas every day. He doesn't believe soda is unhealthy.

    ignoring _____

2. Matt stopped smoking two months ago. Yesterday, he started smoking again.

    _____

3. Isabel eats a lot of junk food. She knows it is unhealthy, but she keeps eating it.

    _____

Tip for Success

Notice: You can use gerunds after the verbs *stop*, *start*, *begin*, and *keep*. See Unit 4, page 56.

4. Sun-Hee wants to get more exercise. She's going to start walking to work. She wants to start an exercise class, too.

    _____

5. Mary stopped drinking coffee two months ago. Now she drinks tea every morning.

    _____

6. Carlos started a diet this week. He's eating more fruits and vegetables.

    _____

Remember: When you read, notice the pronouns. Ask yourself, "What does this pronoun refer to?" Review the Reading Skill box in Unit 7, page 100.

C. Read these sentences from Reading 1. What does the underlined pronoun refer to? Circle the words and draw an arrow.

1. To change a habit, you have to change your behavior. It is always difficult at the beginning.

2. You ignore the problem or don't pay attention to <u>it</u>.

3. You know your habit is unhealthy, but you don't have a plan to change <u>it</u>.

4. Remember, habits take a long time to make, so <u>they</u> take a long time to change.

WHAT DO YOU THINK?

A. Why are these habits unhealthy? Match the habit with the reason.

Habit

1. I want to quit smoking _b_

2. I want to drink less coffee ____

3. I want to get more sleep ____

4. I want to work less ____

5. I want to stop drinking soda ____

6. I want to get more exercise ____

Reason

a. because my body needs to rest.

b. because it is bad for my lungs.

c. because it has unhealthy ingredients.

d. because my body needs to be strong.

e. because I need time to relax.

f. because it has a lot of caffeine.

B. Answer the questions. Write complete sentences.

1. What habit do you want to change? _____

_____

2. Why is it difficult to change this habit? _____

_____

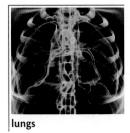

lungs

READING 2 | Dr. Lee on Health

VOCABULARY

Here are some words from Reading 2. Read the sentences. What do the bold words mean? Circle *a* or *b*.

1. I **am addicted to** coffee. When I don't drink coffee, I get a headache.
   a. like
   b. can't stop drinking

2. At the end of a long workday, Matt feels **exhausted**. He just wants to rest.
   a. extremely tired
   b. talkative

3. I have two tests this week. I feel a lot of **stress**.
   a. calm
   b. worry

4. I want to **break** my habit of drinking sodas. They have too much sugar.
   a. start
   b. stop

5. She drinks water **instead of** juice. Water is healthier.
   a in addition to
   b. to replace

6. My friend is very heavy. He needs to **lose weight**.
   a. become thinner
   b. become heavier

7. I want to give you some money, but **unfortunately** I don't have any.
   a. sadly
   b. happily

8. When I cook, I don't use a recipe. I like to **create** my own dishes.
   a. name
   b. make

PREVIEW READING 2

In this newspaper article, a doctor answers questions from readers. Scan the reading for names. Complete the sentences.

1. _____ wants to lose weight.

2. _____ gives advice to readers.

3. _____ plays a lot of video games.

Dr. Lee on Health

Sleepless Sam

1 Dear Dr. Lee,

I am **addicted to** video games. I can't stop playing them. I don't feel tired at night because I love playing games. I usually stay up until 3 a.m. I never get enough sleep! During the day, I am **exhausted** and I fall asleep in class. I feel a lot of **stress** because I am behind in my schoolwork. What's your advice?

Sleepless Sam

2 Dear Sam,

Your problem isn't unusual. Many people are addicted to video games. How can you **break** this habit? First, you should make a plan. Begin to make changes slowly. For example, if you usually play games five hours a day, you could play four hours a day for the first week. The next week, you could play three hours a day. Your goal should be one hour a day of video games. Second, replace video games with a different activity. You could spend time with friends **instead of** with video games. You could turn off your computer at 9:00 and read a good book. You will want to play video games, but you need to break this habit. Good luck!

Dr. Lee

3 Dear Dr. Lee,

I love the TV show *The Biggest Loser*. Contestants[1] on the show try to **lose weight**, and most of them are successful. They reach their goals. I want to lose 20 pounds. Will the show's diet plan work for me?

Mary

4 Dear Mary,

The contestants on *The Biggest Loser* lose a lot of weight quickly. Diet and exercise experts plan everything the contestants eat and do. But what happens after the show? **Unfortunately**, most contestants gain weight again. Why? After the

The Biggest Loser

show, contestants don't exercise five to six hours a day. They often return to unhealthy lifestyles. If you want to lose weight, there are no quick and easy diet plans. It takes time to lose weight and learn new habits. You should **create** your own diet plan. Remember your goal: a healthy lifestyle.

Dr. Lee

[1] **contestants:** people in a contest or game show

COMPREHENSION CHECK

A. Circle the correct answer.

Tip for Success

In the Reading, Sam calls himself "sleepless." Noun + *-less* means not having something. For example, *sleepless* means not having sleep. Other words with *-less* are *thoughtless* and *useless*.

1. Sam is tired during the day because he ___.
   a. stays up late
   b. falls asleep in class
   c. feels a lot of stress
   d. doesn't drink coffee

2. Dr. Lee thinks that Sam should ___.
   a. get up early
   b. change his habit quickly
   c. play different games
   d. break his habit

3. Mary writes to Dr. Lee because she wants to ___.
   a. be on a TV program
   b. meet Dr. Lee
   c. lose weight
   d. gain weight

4. Dr. Lee says that Mary should ___.
   a. create her own diet plan
   b. go on the TV show
   c. lose 20 pounds
   d. not try to lose weight

B. Answer the questions.

1. Sam isn't tired at night. Why?

   _____

2. Why is Sam behind in his schoolwork?

   _____

3. According to Dr. Lee, does Sam have a common problem?

   _____

4. What are the two suggestions for Sam?

   _____

5. How much weight does Mary want to lose?

   _____

6. Why do contestants gain weight after the TV program?

   _____

 **WHAT DO YOU THINK?**

A. Discuss the questions with a partner.

1. What unhealthy habit do you have? Why is it important to change the habit?

2. Do you have a goal? What is it?

3. Do you have a plan? What is it?

Tip **Critical Thinking**

In Question 1 of Activity B, you have to **transfer** your knowledge from Reading 1 to think about Reading 2. When you use information in a new way, it helps you to understand and remember it better.

B. Think about both Reading 1 and 2 and answer these questions in your notebook. Use complete sentences.

1. In Reading 1, there are six stages of change. Think about the people in Reading 2. Which stage is Sam at? Which stage is Mary at?

2. Which habit in Reading 2 is harder to break? Why? In your opinion, how long will it take to change each habit?

Building Vocabulary | Collocations

Collocations are words that we often use together. For example, we can use the verbs *gain* or *lose* with the noun *weight*:

> I often **gain weight** during the holidays.
> I usually **lose weight** during the summer.

Reduce and *lose* have similar meanings, but you don't say "I often reduce weight."

Verb + noun collocations

break a habit	It's hard to **break the habit** of smoking.
gain/lose weight	I want to **lose weight**.
set a goal	I **set a goal** to run a mile in 10 minutes.
reach a goal	Next year, I will **reach my goal**. I will become a nurse.

Verb + preposition collocations

cut down on	I'm too heavy. I need to **cut down on** desserts.
be behind in	I **am behind in** my school work.
go off	Last weekend, I **went off** my diet. I had dessert every night.
go on	I **will go on** a new diet tomorrow.

A. Complete the sentences. Use words and collocations from the Building Vocabulary box.

1. I will _____ to graduate from a four-year college.

2. I will _____ in about five years.

3. My doctor said I should _____. I am too heavy.

4. My house is messy. I am very busy this week, so I

   _____ my housecleaning chores.

5. I often fall asleep in front of the TV. I need to _____ that

   _____.

6. I'm going to _____ video games. I'll only play

   for an hour a day.

B. Answer the questions. Then ask and answer questions with a partner.

1. What habit do you want to break? What do you want to stop doing?

   _____

   _____

2. What goal do you want to reach this year?

   _____

   _____

3. What goal can you set for learning vocabulary?

   _____

   _____

4. What are you behind in right now? (housework, schoolwork, email)

   _____

   _____

   A: What habit do you want to break?
   B: I want to stop watching TV late at night.

I will reach my goal.

1. A modal comes before a base form verb. Modals can be affirmative or negative.*

   I **should eat** more fruit.　　　Sometimes I **can't sleep** at night.
   　modal　base verb　　　　　　　　modal　base verb

   Don't put an **-s** at the end of the verb.

   ✓ Correct: He **can eat** a whole pizza.
   ✗ Incorrect: He can eats a whole pizza.

2. Use *can/can't* to talk about possibility or ability.

   Some habits **can** take a year to change.　　She **can't** sleep at night.

3. Use *could* to make a polite suggestion.

   You **could** come with me to my exercise class.

4. Use *should/shouldn't* to give advice.

   They **should** eat more fruit.　　　　They **shouldn't** eat junk food.

   *The full forms of *shouldn't* and *can't* are *should not* and *cannot*.

A. Read this paragraph from Reading 2. Underline the modals *could* or *should* + verb. Label each modal as *S* (suggestion) or *A* (advice).

　　　Many people are addicted to video games. . . . How can you break
this habit? First, you <u>should make</u> a plan. Begin to make changes slowly.
For example, if you usually play games five hours a day, you could play
four hours a day for the first week. The next week, you could play three
hours a day. Your goal should be one hour a day of video games. Second,
replace video games with a different activity. You could spend time with
friends instead of with video games. You could turn off your computer
at 9:00 and read a good book. You will want to play video games, but
you need to break this habit. Good luck!

I love potato chips.

B. Complete the sentences with *can* or *can't*.

1. If I eat one potato chip, I _____ stop. I want to eat more.

2. It's difficult to break a habit, but you _____ do it.

3. People _____ become addicted to soda.

4. Most people _____ lose weight when they exercise every day.

5. I _____ speak loudly today. I have a bad cold.

C. Complete the sentences with *should* or *shouldn't*.

1. Some experts say we _____ drink eight glasses of water a day.

2. You _____ drink more than three cups of coffee a day.

3. It's very cold outside. You _____ wear a jacket.

4. It's really hot. We _____ go outside right now.

5. During class, you _____ pay attention to the teacher.

6. David _____ change his lifestyle. He needs to eat less junk food.

7. Anna feels a lot of stress. She _____ work so hard.

8. You _____ start smoking. You will become addicted to it.

D. Read the statements. Write polite suggestions with *could*.

1. I'm having trouble with my homework.

   Suggestion: _You could ask your teacher for help._

2. I need to gain weight.

   Suggestion: _____

3. I need to lose weight.

   Suggestion: _____

4. I need to relax.

   Suggestion: _____

5. I want to join a health club.

   Suggestion: _____

In a paragraph, the topic sentence introduces the topic. Supporting sentences give information about the topic sentence.

1. All supporting sentences should **connect to the paragraph topic**. When you edit your writing, delete (cross out) sentences that do not connect to the topic.

> Many children are addicted to foods with sugar. Their favorite foods are candy, cake, cookies, and ice cream. ~~I love chocolate ice cream~~. Children want desserts with sugar after every meal.

In this example, the topic is "children addicted to sugar." The sentence "I love chocolate ice cream" is about the writer's favorite food. It is not about children in general.

2. Supporting sentences can **give examples**. Introduce your examples with *For example* and *For instance*.

> Everyone has a few unhealthy habits. **For example**, maybe you eat too much junk food. This is a common habit in today's lifestyle.

3. Supporting sentences can **give reasons** with *because*. Reasons explain your ideas.

> Many children are addicted to food with sugar. Children can get sick **because** they eat sweet things instead of fruits and vegetables.

A. Read each paragraph. Delete the supporting sentence that is <u>not</u> about the paragraph topic.

1.

> My grandmother is 75 years old, and she is very healthy. She is very careful about her diet. She never eats too much food, so she doesn't gain weight. She is a wonderful cook. She goes for a walk every morning. Her daily habits keep her healthy.

2.

My older sister feels a lot of stress about school. She worries about her classes. She thinks her grades will be bad, but her grades are always good. My grades are OK. My sister studies every night until midnight. I think she should relax for a while every day.

B. Write examples. Start with *For example* or *For instance.*

1. Many people love sweet foods. _For example, most people have sweet_ _snacks and eat dessert after dinner._

2. Some young people are addicted to their cell phones. _____

   _____

3. Most diets don't work after a month or so. _____

   _____

4. It's easy to exercise a little every day. _____

   _____

5. A student's lifestyle creates stress. _____

   _____

C. Complete each statement. Give a reason with *because.*

1. You shouldn't eat too many sweet foods _because too much sugar is_ _bad for you_____.

2. You should eat fruit and vegetables _____.

   _____.

3. You shouldn't watch so much TV _____.

   _____.

4. You should walk to school _____.

   _____.

5. You should stay home when you are sick _____.

   _____.

In this assignment, you write a paragraph about how to change an unhealthy habit. Think about the Unit Question, "How can you change an unhealthy habit?" and use the Self-Assessment checklist on page 129.

A. BRAINSTORM With a partner, discuss the two questions. For each question, think of several possible answers. Write ideas in your notebook.

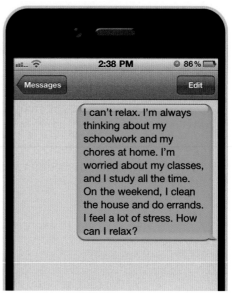

B. WRITE Choose one question from Activity A. Write a paragraph to answer the question. Follow these steps:

1. Write a topic sentence. Include the topic and your main idea about it.

2. Write the body of the paragraph. In your supporting sentences, include reasons and examples. Don't include sentences that do not support the topic sentence.

3. Write a concluding sentence.

C. REVISE Answer the questions about your supporting sentences. Then revise and rewrite your paragraph.

1. How many supporting sentences do you have? Can you add another supporting sentence?

2. Do you introduce at least one example with *for example* or *for instance*?

3. Do you have one sentence with *because* to give a reason?

D. **EDIT** Review your paragraph and complete the Self-Assessment checklist. Make any final changes. Be prepared to hand in your work or discuss it in class.

SELF-ASSESSMENT		
Yes	**No**	
☐	☐	Is your capitalization and punctuation correct?
☐	☐	Are there any collocations or new vocabulary from the unit?
☐	☐	Do you use the modals *can*, *could*, and *should* correctly?
☐	☐	Is there a supporting sentence with for *example*, *for instance*, or *because*?

Track Your Success

Circle the words you learned in this unit.

Nouns
behavior 🔑
diet
expert 🔑 AWL
goal 🔑 AWL
lifestyle
stress 🔑 AWL

Verbs
become 🔑
break 🔑

create 🔑 AWL
give up

Adjectives
addicted (to)
discouraged
exhausted

Adverb
unfortunately 🔑

Preposition
instead (of) 🔑

Phrases/Collocations
be behind in
break a habit
cut down on (dessert)
gain weight
go off (a diet)
go on (a diet)
lose weight
pay attention
reach a goal
set a goal

🔑 Oxford 2000 keywords
AWL Academic Word List

Check (✓) the skills you learned. If you need more work on a skill, refer to the page(s) in parentheses.

READING ●	I can identify pronoun references. (p. 117)
VOCABULARY ●	I can use collocations. (p. 122)
GRAMMAR ●	I can use modals *can*, *could*, and *should*. (p. 124)
WRITING ●	I can give examples and reasons to support ideas. (p. 126)
LEARNING OUTCOME ●	I can write a paragraph about how to change a bad habit. (p. 128)

Unit QUESTION

Why do people live in cities?

PREVIEW THE UNIT

A What words describe your city or town? Circle three
words. Compare your answers with your classmates.

beautiful	clean	expensive	quiet
boring	dirty	friendly	safe
busy	exciting	inexpensive	ugly

B Look at the photo. What are the people doing? Does this
look like an interesting place?

C Discuss the Unit Question above with your classmates.

Listen to *The Q Classroom*, Track 21, to hear other answers.

READING 1 | Why Do People Love Their Cities?

VOCABULARY

Here are some words from Reading 1. Read each sentence. Then write each bold word next to the correct definition.

1. The newspaper did a **survey** about public schools. They interviewed about 20,000 people.

2. One **characteristic** of a good city is friendly people.

3. Last night two men robbed a bank and took a lot of money. It was a serious **crime**.

4. The **economy** in my city is good. There are many jobs, and the stores are full of customers.

5. There are about 55 **residents** in my apartment building.

6. Trains, buses, and subways are part of the **public** transportation in the city.

7. People in this small town **welcome** visitors. They enjoy showing visitors their town.

8. My grandfather is an **immigrant** from China. He was born in China.

My grandfather is from China.

a. _____ (*noun*) an illegal activity—it is against the law

b. _____ (*adjective*) for everyone

c. _____ (*verb*) to be friendly when someone arrives

d. _____ (*noun*) a special quality—it makes a person or thing different from others

e. _____ (*noun*) a person—he or she moves to a new country and lives there

f. _____ (*noun*) money and business in a place (city, country, world)

g. _____ (*noun*) people—they live in a city, neighborhood, or building

h. _____ (*noun*) a list of questions about a topic

PREVIEW READING 1

This article is about characteristics of great cities. Which characteristics are important to you? Number the characteristics from 1 (most important) to 6 (least important).

____ lots of parks

____ good schools and colleges

____ good jobs

____ good public transportation

____ nice, inexpensive apartments and houses

____ fun entertainment and events

Track 22 **Read the article.**

Why Do People Love Their Cities?

1   What is the best city in the world? Every year, Mercer Consulting does a **survey** of over 400 cities around the world. They look at ten **characteristics** of cities, including **crime**, the **economy**, the cost of housing, and more. In 2010, they reported that Vienna, Austria was the best city in the world. Other great cities were Vancouver, Canada; Sydney, Australia; Singapore; San Francisco, the United States; and Dubai, the United Arab Emirates.

Vienna, Austria

2   When **residents** love their city, the city grows and the economy improves. The Mercer study is interesting, but it doesn't answer this question: Why do residents love their cities? Many city leaders around the world wanted an answer to this question. In 2008, Gallup and the Knight Foundation started a new survey to answer it. They interviewed 43,000 adults in 25 cities in the United States. Experts found three important answers to the question. These three answers were the same in all 25 cities.

Places for social activities

3   Restaurants, theaters, museums, and
community events are all places for social
activities. Residents can enjoy spending time
with friends and family members in the city. In
addition, **public** spaces are important. Public
spaces can be parks, plazas, and downtown
areas. In public spaces, residents can sit,
eat lunch, relax, or meet with friends.

Plaza Mayor, Salamanca, Spain

Beauty

4   The appearance of a city is very important.
Parks, trees, and flowers add beauty to a city.
Public art (for example, statues, fountains,
and paintings) also adds beauty to a city.

Openness

5   Openness means the friendliness
of a city. Does the city **welcome** new
residents? Does it welcome **immigrants**
from other countries? Does it welcome
people of different ages and interests?

Bryant Park, New York City, U.S.

6   When residents love their city, the city
economy grows. When the economy grows,
there are more jobs. But jobs are not the
most important thing for residents. They do
not love their city because of good jobs, good
highways, or good schools. They love their
cities because of places for social activities,
beauty, and openness. City leaders should pay
attention to these characteristics in their cities.

Vancouver, Canada

COMPREHENSION CHECK

A. Read each sentence. Where can you find this information in the article? Write the paragraph number.

___ a. A survey asked: Why do residents love their cities?

___ b. Residents like a welcoming city.

___ c. Social activities are important to residents.

___ d. Good highways don't make a city great.

___ e. A painting can be public art.

___ f. Mercer Consulting looks for the best city in the world each year.

___ g. They interviewed 43,000 adults.

___ h. Vienna was the best city in 2010.

___ i. City leaders should make sure their city has places for social activities, beauty, and openness.

B. Look at Activity A. Which sentences are main ideas? Which are supporting ideas? Write the letters.

1. Main ideas: _____

2. Supporting ideas: _____

Q? WHAT DO YOU THINK?

A. Write three cities or towns in the chart. Then give each city a number from 1 to 5 (1 = very bad, 5 = very good) for each characteristic in the chart.

Tip Critical Thinking

Activity A asks you to **evaluate** different cities. When you evaluate, you use information and opinions to make decisions about things.

City or town:			
Places for social activities			
Beauty			
Openness			

B. Work with a partner. Compare your charts. Discuss these questions.

1. Which city in Activity A is your favorite? Why?

2. Which city is best for students and young adults? Which is best for families with young children? Which is best for older people? Why?

| Reading Skill | Building reading fluency | |

Reading fluency means how quickly and easily you read. It is important to increase your reading speed. Here are two ways to build your reading fluency.

1. Move your eyes across each line and down the article. Keep your eyes moving. Don't stop for words you don't know.

2. Remember: You don't have to understand every word in an article.
   - The first time you read, look for the main ideas.
   - The second time you read, pay more attention to the details and the vocabulary.

Sometimes you read an article three or four times. Each time, try to read it more quickly. When you read something several times, you can increase your reading fluency.

A. Do three timed readings of Reading 1 on pages 133–134. Each time, read for 30 seconds. Follow these steps.

1. When your teacher says "Start," read from the beginning of Reading 1.

2. When your teacher says "Stop," write a small *1* exactly where you stop.

3. Do the timed reading two more times. Each time, start at the beginning. The second time, write a *2* where you stop. The third time, write a *3*.

4. Did you read more each time? Did you increase your reading fluency?

B. Nine words are missing from this paragraph. Read the paragraph fluently, without stopping. Then circle the correct answer to complete each main idea below.

Residents of a city are interested in the _____ of life in a city. They want to live happily and _____ in a city. For example, places for social activities and events, public areas and parks, natural beauty, and openness are all important for residents. But tourists are _____ in different things. Tourists want to see _____ things such as _____ monuments and famous places. They want to experience the most _____ places in a city. Easy transportation, friendly people, and _____ experiences are all important to tourists. For this _____, cities with the best lifestyle are not always the top tourist cities. And the top tourist _____ are not always the best places to live.

1. This article discusses ____.
   a. residents
   b. tourists and residents
   c. residents and friendly people
   d. immigrants

2. Residents and tourists are interested in ____ things in a city.
   a. the same
   b. famous
   c. different
   d. fun

3. The city with the best lifestyle is ____ the top tourist city.
   a. usually
   b. always
   c. never
   d. not always

Prague, Czech Republic

READING 2 | First Impressions

VOCABULARY

Here are some words from Reading 2. Read the sentences. What do the bold words mean? Circle *a* or *b*.

1. There are many **complaints** about this restaurant. The food is not very good.
   a. comments from unhappy people
   b. comments from happy people

2. In my **opinion**, the city lifestyle is wonderful and exciting.
   a. a thought about something
   b. a report about a topic

3. There are many **international** students at this university. Students come from all over the world.
   a. from different countries
   b. intelligent

4. This park **seems** very safe. There are a lot of families with children.
   a. looks like it is
   b. smells like it is

5. The air in the city is dirty and polluted. It needs to **improve**.
   a. get worse
   b. get better

6. My first **impression** of the neighborhood was good. I liked it because there were many beautiful trees.
   a. idea or feeling
   b. town or city

7. On weekends, I buy fresh fruit at a farmers' **market** downtown. Each farmer sells a good variety of fruits.
   a. place to eat food
   b. place to shop for things

8. This museum is very expensive. I'm very **surprised**. I thought it was free.
   a. serious feeling about something
   b. feeling when something unusual happens

PREVIEW READING 2

This online article is about readers' first impressions of Berlin, Germany. Discuss this city with a partner. What do you already know about Berlin?

First Impressions

1   Some long-time residents of Berlin have **complaints** about their city. Last week, we invited some of our newer residents to give their thoughts and **opinions**.

Mei

2   I am from Taiwan, and I moved here two years ago. I'm studying engineering at Humboldt University. Berlin is very **international**. That is its best characteristic. There are students and professors from all over the world. During my first year here, many students didn't **seem** friendly toward new people. I was shy at the beginning because my German wasn't very good. When my German **improved**, I tried to talk to other students more. After several months, I made a few good friends. Then I started to enjoy the city with my friends. My first **impression** was not very good. People seemed unfriendly. But now I have a good opinion of Berlin, and I enjoy studying here.

Humboldt University

Tala

3   I am from the Philippines, and I moved here with my family five years ago. I really don't like cold weather, so at first, I was unhappy. But people in this city don't stay inside in the winter. For example, last December, I visited the outdoor **markets** with my parents. It was cold, and it was dark at 3:30 p.m. But the markets were so colorful! My family and I walked around for hours. We went to many shops. We enjoyed the beautiful lights. Everyone was outside, having fun! When we were too cold, we stopped for a hot drink at a café. Later in the evening, there was a free concert. On that winter night, the city was exciting. The next day, I went ice skating with my friends. From the big outside skating rink, there was a beautiful view of the city. Now I think differently about the cold winter months.

outdoor markets

Pedro

4   My first impression of Berlin was very good. This city really welcomes bicyclists, and that is very unusual. I love biking, but it can be dangerous in a city. On my first weekend in Berlin, I biked all over the city. There are special red bike paths everywhere, and they are very safe. I was really **surprised**. Also, I explored the beautiful city parks and gardens.

red bike paths in Berlin

COMPREHENSION CHECK

A. Read the statements. Write *T* (true) or *F* (false). Then correct each false statement to make it true.

____ 1. Mei moved to Berlin five years ago.

____ 2. Mei didn't speak German very well when she arrived.

____ 3. Mei doesn't like studying in Berlin now.

____ 4. Residents of Berlin enjoy spending time outside in the winter.

____ 5. Tala didn't like the outdoor markets.

____ 6. Tala enjoyed skiing in Berlin.

____ 7. Pedro enjoys running in the city parks in Berlin.

____ 8. The bike paths in Berlin are red.

B. Answer the questions.

1. What did you learn about Berlin? Write three things.

_____

2. How is Berlin similar to your city?

_____

3. How is Berlin different from your city?

_____

Q WHAT DO YOU THINK?

A. Imagine that Mei, Tala, and Pedro are coming to your city or town. Complete the chart. Then discuss your answers with a partner.

Mei should see . . . because . . .   I can take her to . . . .

	Where should you take this visitor?	What can you show your visitor? Why?
Mei		
Tala		
Pedro		

B. Think about both Reading 1 and Reading 2. Answer the questions in your notebook. Then discuss them with a partner.

1. Think about the three characteristics of a good city. Which characteristic is the most important to you? Why?

2. In your opinion, how can your city improve? What does it need to do? Give examples and suggestions.

Building Vocabulary · Using the dictionary web

pollution

When you learn a new word, use your dictionary to learn other words in the same **word family**. For example, look up *pollution* in your dictionary. You will find the verb *pollute* above it. To review word families, see Unit 2, page 24.

pol·lute /pə'lut/ *verb* (**pol·lutes, pol·lut·ing, pol·lut·ed**)
to make the air, rivers, etc. dirty and dangerous: *Many of our rivers are polluted with chemicals from factories.*

pol·lu·tion /pə'luʃn/ *noun* [*noncount*]
1 the action of making the air, rivers, etc. dirty and dangerous: *We must stop the **pollution of** our beaches.*
2 dirty and dangerous chemicals, gases, etc. that harm the environment: *Our rivers are full of pollution.* ⊃ Look at the note at **environment**.

All dictionary entries are from the *Oxford Basic American Dictionary for learners of English*. © Oxford University Press 2011.

A. Complete the chart. Use your dictionary. (An **X** means that a word doesn't exist or that you don't need to know it.)

	Noun	Verb	Adjective
1.		appear	
2.		X	beautiful
3.			interesting; interested
4.	X		modern
5.		X	public
6.	openness		open
7.	pollution		
8.			relaxing; relaxed
9.		X	safe
10.	society		social

B. Complete the sentences. Use the correct noun, verb, or adjective from Activity A. More than one answer may be correct.

1. I like to _____relax_____ in the park. It is a _____ place.

2. Our city's garden is _____ in the springtime. There are many colorful flowers.

3. Cars _____ the air and make it dirty. Cars cause _____ in the city.

4. The post office and the library are _____ buildings. Those buildings are open to the _____ six days a week.

5. Our airport is very old. Next year, the city will _____ it with free Internet service, new furniture, and new shops.

6. I'm a very talkative and _____ person. I like to _____ with my friends in the cafeteria after class.

7. I live in a very _____ neighborhood. I don't worry about my _____.

8. On Friday, the stores _____ at 10 a.m. and close at 9 p.m.

WRITING

Past of *be*

Use the past of *be* to identify and describe people and things in the past.

Affirmative and negative statements

subject	*be*	*(not)*	
I	**was**		happy in Hong Kong.
You We They	**were**	**(not)**	at the outdoor market.
He She It	**was**		in the public garden.

- You can contract negative statements:

  was not = **wasn't**   were not = **weren't**

Yes/No questions

be	subject			Short answers	*yes*	*no*
Was	the apartment	expensive?			Yes, it **was.**	No, it **wasn't.**
Were	the streets	safe?			Yes, they **were.**	No, they **weren't.**

Information questions

wh- word	*be*	subject		Answers
Who	**was**	the actor?		Matt Damon **was** the actor.
What	**were**	the questions	about?	They **were** about cities.
Where	**was**	the museum?		It **was** near the park.

Simple past affirmative statements

The simple past describes completed actions in the past.

The simple past verb form is the same for all subjects.

Last summer, we **visited** Miami.

My cousins **welcomed** us into their home.

> The train **stopped** at the station.
> Ana **stayed** home and studied for the test.

Spelling of simple past verbs	
Add -*ed* after most verbs. Add -*d* after verbs that end in -*e*.	travel**ed**, walk**ed** welcome**d**, improve**d**
If a <u>one-syllable</u> verb ends in vowel + consonant, double the consonant and add -*ed*.	plan**ned**, stop**ped**
If the verb ends in a consonant + -*y*, change the *y* to *i* and add -*ed*.	stud**ied**, tr**ied**
If the verb ends in vowel + -*y*, add -*ed*.	play**ed**, stay**ed**

A. Complete each sentence with *was*, *were*, *wasn't*, or *weren't*.

The city was very clean.

1. The city _____was_____ very clean. There _____ any trash in the streets.

2. The beautiful sky _____ clear and blue. The air _____ polluted.

3. The taxi _____ very expensive. Next time, I will take the bus instead of a taxi.

4. The city residents _____ worried about the increase in crime.

5. We _____ exhausted after the trip. The roads _____ very crowded and traffic moved slowly.

6. Last year, the economy in my area _____ very bad. It's better now.

7. Yesterday I answered some survey questions. They _____ about apartments.

8. I _____ happy about my new office. It was very dark.

B. Complete the two paragraphs about Dubai.

This first paragraph is a general description of Dubai. Use the simple present.

Dubai _____ (be) a very impressive, modern city. It

_____ (have) some of the tallest buildings in the world,
2

and the shopping malls, hotels, and restaurants _____ (be)
3

all very new—and expensive! Dubai _____ (be) on a
4

peninsula, and it _____ (have) beautiful beaches. The
5

weather _____ (be) very sunny and warm.
6

This paragraph is about the writer's first impressions of Dubai. Use the simple past.

My wife and I _____ (move) to Dubai in the United
7

Arab Emirates last year. My first impression of Dubai _____ (be)
8

good. The people _____ (be) very welcoming and
9

_____ (answer) our questions. On the weekend, we
10

_____ (walk) down narrow streets in the old market area.
11

However, the daytime temperatures _____ (be) very hot. I
12

_____ (try) to stay inside with the air conditioning.
13

C. Write the words in the correct order to make questions. Then ask and answer the questions with a partner.

1. hot / it / was / yesterday ?

   _____

2. this school / your / what / was / of / first impression ?

   _____

3. people / were / friendly ?

   _____

4. last time / in class / were / how many / students ?

   _____

5. school building / last night / was / the / open ?

_____

6. your teacher / who / last year / was ?

_____

 In this assignment, you write two paragraphs describing a city you visited. Think about the Unit Question, "Why do people live in cities?" and use the Self-Assessment checklist on page 147.

A. **BRAINSTORM** Think about a city you visited. Complete the T-chart below. Then share your ideas with a partner.

Places, parks, and shops in the city	Adjectives to describe the city

 Tip for Success

Some verbs have irregular forms. Here are some useful irregular past verbs.

go	went
see	saw
have	had
buy	bought

B. **WRITE** Write two paragraphs about a city. First, describe the city. Use simple present. Then describe your visit. What did you do? Use simple past. Use the paragraphs in Activity B on page 145 as examples.

Skill Review   **Supporting your ideas**

Remember: All supporting sentences should connect to the paragraph topic. Support your ideas with examples and reasons. Review the Writing Skill box in Unit 8, page 126.

C. **REVISE** Read your paragraph to a partner. Discuss these questions. Then revise and rewrite your paragraph.

1. Is there a description of the city? What else can you say about the city?

2. What was interesting about the visit? What else did you do?

D. **EDIT** Review your paragraph and complete the Self-Assessment checklist. Make any final changes. Be prepared to hand in your work or discuss it in class.

SELF-ASSESSMENT		
Yes	No	
☐	☐	Does every sentence have a subject and a verb?
☐	☐	Does every sentence start with a capital letter?
☐	☐	Does every sentence end with a period?
☐	☐	Check every verb. Is it the correct tense? Is it spelled correctly?

Track Your Success

Circle the words you learned in this unit.

Nouns
appearance 🔑
beauty 🔑
characteristic 🔑
complaint 🔑
crime 🔑
economy 🔑 AWL
immigrant AWL
impression 🔑
interest 🔑
market 🔑
openness
opinion 🔑
pollution 🔑

public 🔑
relaxation AWL
resident AWL
safety 🔑
society 🔑
survey AWL

Verbs
appear 🔑
improve 🔑
interest 🔑
modernize
open 🔑
pollute

relax 🔑 AWL
seem 🔑
socialize
welcome 🔑

Adjectives
international 🔑
open 🔑
polluted
public 🔑
relaxed 🔑
relaxing AWL
social 🔑
surprised 🔑

🔑 Oxford 2000 keywords
AWL Academic Word List

Check (✓) the skills you learned. If you need more work on a skill, refer to the page(s) in parentheses.

READING	●	I can build my reading fluency. (p. 136)
VOCABULARY	●	I can use the dictionary to identify word families. (p. 141)
GRAMMAR	●	I can use the past of *be* and the simple past with regular past verbs. (p. 143)
WRITING	●	I can give examples to support ideas. (p. 146)
LEARNING OUTCOME	●	I can write two paragraphs describing a city I visited. (p. 146)

UNIT **10**

Milestones

READING ● building reading fluency
VOCABULARY ● using the dictionary: definitions
GRAMMAR ● simple past with regular and irregular verbs
WRITING ● showing sequence

Unit QUESTION

What events change our lives?

PREVIEW THE UNIT

Ⓐ Look at these important life events. In what order do they usually happen? Number them from 1 to 8. Discuss your answers with a partner.

____ get a job   ____ move away from home
____ get married   ____ start school
____ graduate from college   ____ buy a home
____ graduate from high school   ____ start a family

Ⓑ Look at the photo. Where are the people? What is happening?

Ⓒ Discuss the Unit Question above with your classmates.

🔊 Listen to *The Q Classroom*, Track 24, to hear other answers.

149

READING 1 | A Promise to Children

VOCABULARY

Here are some words from Reading 1. Read the definitions. Then complete the sentences below.

> **challenging** (*adjective*) difficult
> **continue** (*verb*) to not stop doing something
> **decide** (*verb*) to choose
> **dream** (*noun*) something good that you hope for
> **even** (*adverb*) used to show something surprising
> **opportunity** (*noun*) a chance to do something
> **organization** (*noun*) a group of people—they work together to meet a goal
> **promise** (*verb*) to say that you will do or will not do something

1. Can you loan me a little money? I _____ to pay you back tomorrow.

2. My new job is very _____. I need to learn several new computer programs.

3. Did you _____ to take a trip? When do you need to make your decision?

4. Immigrants first came to the United States hundreds of years ago. Today, immigrants _____ to move to the United States.

5. Hassan's _____ is to become a restaurant owner someday.

6. I belong to a neighborhood _____. We meet once a month to talk about problems in our community.

7. _____ in winter, Dubai is sometimes very hot.

8. When I was young, I enjoyed working at my father's store. It wasn't hard, but I learned a lot about business. It was a great

_____ for me.

PREVIEW READING 1

Tip for Success

Before you read, look at the photos. Read the captions under the photos for information about the topic.

This is an article about a man named John Wood. Look at the photos and read the captions. Then answer the question.

What do you think John Wood did? Check (✓) your answer.

☐ a. He was a tourist in Nepal. Later, he built schools.

☐ b. He was a mountain climber. Later, he became a teacher.

☐ c. He loved hiking in Nepal, so he decided to live there.

| Skill Review | Building reading fluency |

Remember: You can increase your reading speed. Read an article several times. The first time, read for the main idea. The second time, read for details. The third time, increase your reading fluency. Don't stop for new words. Review the Reading Skill box in Unit 9, page 136.

Track 25   **Read the article.**

A Promise to Children

Before 1999, John Wood was a successful businessman. But that year, John Wood made a promise, and it changed his life completely.

1   In 1998, John Wood was an executive at Microsoft in Australia. He was only 35 years old, but he had an important job with a high salary and long hours. He needed a vacation, so he went hiking for three weeks in the Himalayan Mountains in Nepal. During his hike, he met a teacher from a small village. The teacher invited Wood on a tour of

Kathmandu Valley, Himalayas, Nepal

his school, and Wood was shocked[1]. There were only 20 books for hundreds of students, but they were not textbooks.

---

[1] **shocked:** feeling surprised in a bad way

They were tour books and novels[2] from other hikers. As Wood left the village, the school principal said: "Perhaps, sir, you will someday come back with books."

2   The visit to the village changed Wood and he made a promise to himself: return to Nepal with books. He started to ask his friends and family for help. Later in 1998, Microsoft moved Wood to a job in China. **Even** in China, he **continued** to think about Nepal and collect books. In 1999, Wood and his father brought thousands of books to the village. In the same year, Wood **decided** to leave his job at Microsoft. He was a successful businessman, but his new **dream** was to bring books and education to children around the world. He wanted all children to have the **opportunity** to be successful like him. In 2000, he started an **organization**, Room to Read.

3   At first, it was **challenging**. He had no salary, and the organization's office was in his home. He had to raise a lot of money and hire good people. But Wood had strong business skills, and he was very organized. Many people became excited about Wood's dream, and Room to Read grew quickly.

4   In the first ten years, Room to Read helped five million children and built more than 1,000 schools and 11,000 libraries in Bangladesh, Cambodia, India, Laos, Nepal, South Africa, Sri Lanka, Vietnam, and Zambia. Also, the organization gave away more than nine million books and created hundreds of children's books in 23 languages. Today, Wood and Room to Read continue to help children in Asia and Africa. Their goal is to help educate 10 million children by 2015. Wood also published his first children's book in 2010, *Zak the Yak with Books on His Back.* Where does the story take place? You guessed it—Nepal.

John Wood in Nepal

---

[2] **novel:** a written story about people and events that are not real

COMPREHENSION CHECK

A. Read the statements. Write *T* (true) or *F* (false). Then correct each false statement to make it true.

_____ 1.   John Wood worked at Microsoft in 1998.

_____ 2.   He moved to Nepal for work.

_____ 3.   He visited a school in Nepal, and it had many books.

_____ 4.   Wood decided to bring books and education to children.

_____ 5. When he started Room to Read, Wood got a large salary.

_____ 6. Room to Read built more than 1,000 schools in the first 10 years.

 Tip for Success

A time line helps you see the important events in the correct order.

B. Complete the time line. Write the letter of each event in the correct place.

a. returned to Nepal with thousands of books	d. left his job at Microsoft
b. wrote a children's book	e. started Room to Read
c. went hiking in Nepal	f. moved to a job in China

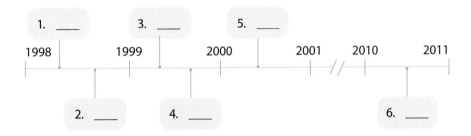

1. _____   3. _____   5. _____

1998   1999   2000   2001   2010   2011

2. _____   4. _____   6. _____

C. What event changed Wood's life in 1998? How do you think this changed the lives of children in villages in Asia and Africa?

_____

_____

_____

Q **WHAT DO YOU THINK?**

A. Which events happened in your life? Check (✓) the boxes. Then compare with a partner.

had an accident

☐ was on a winning sports team   ☐ had an accident

☐ bought something very expensive   ☐ graduated from high school

☐ met an important or special person ☐ applied to college

☐ experienced extreme weather   ☐ attended a different school

☐ visited a different country   ☐ moved to a different home

B. Think about the Unit Question, "What events change our lives?" Discuss the questions in a group.

1. Which event changed your life?

2. When did this event happen?

3. How did it change your life?

READING 2 | An Extraordinary Coach

VOCABULARY

Here are some words from Reading 2. Read each sentence. Then write each bold word next to the correct definition.

1. My mother's business is very **successful**. She has many customers.

2. When my soccer team won the **championship**, I was very excited.

3. She is a **poor** student because she never does her homework.

4. My aunt had a long **career** in education. She was a teacher for 35 years.

5. My dream is to **turn** my garage **into** an exercise room.

6. Mark is a very **strong** tennis player. He almost always wins.

7. I **believe** that good schools are important for children.

8. Carlos is very intelligent. He is the **top** math student in our school.

a. _____ (*adjective*) best

b. _____ (*adjective*) powerful; not weak

c. _____ (*noun*) a job you learn and do for many years

d. _____ (*adjective*) doing something well

e. _____ (*verb phrase*) to change and become different

f. _____ (*adjective*) bad; not very good

g. _____ (*verb*) to think that something is true

h. _____ (*noun*) a competition to find the best team in a sport

This article is about a basketball coach. Which words do you think are in the article? Underline the words.

baseball	court	field	lose	play
players	score	soccer	team	win

Track 26 **Read the article.**

An Extraordinary Coach

1   About 30 years ago, a **successful** young basketball coach made a big decision. At that time, Tara VanDerveer was the coach for the best college basketball team in the U.S.—Ohio State University. The team won 110 games and four **championships** in five years. In 1985, Stanford University asked VanDerveer to be their basketball coach. Her friends and family thought she should stay at Ohio State. Stanford University was one of the best universities in the U.S., but it had a very **poor** basketball team. Her friends asked her, "Why do you want to leave your terrific job? At Ohio State, you have a wonderful **career**. Stanford will never become a great team." But VanDerveer knew she could make a great team, and she wanted to show others.

Tara VanDerveer coaching Stanford players

"It was kind of like the ultimate[1] challenge," VanDerveer says.

2   In 1985, VanDerveer started coaching at Stanford University. Her goal was to **turn** the Stanford players **into** great athletes. At first, the players didn't have very **strong** basketball skills. But VanDerveer was an extraordinary coach, and she **believed** that her players could become winners. She was right. After five years, the team won a national championship. VanDerveer and her Stanford team continued to have many successful years.

3   In 1995, VanDerveer took a one-year break from Stanford. She coached the U.S. women's basketball team in the 1996 Summer Olympics. Her team won the gold medal. After that, VanDerveer wrote a book about her experience. She wrote about her life as a women's basketball coach, and the fight to win the gold medal.

---

[1] **ultimate:** hardest, most difficult

4   Today the Stanford team is one of the best teams in the country. In 2010, VanDerveer celebrated the 800th win in her career as a coach. She is happy about her decision to move to Stanford. She enjoys coaching some of the most intelligent basketball players in the country and turning them into **top** athletes.

VanDerveer at the 1996 Summer Olympics

COMPREHENSION CHECK

A. Read the sentences. Number them in the correct order from 1 to 6.

_____ a.   She decided to accept the job at Stanford University.

_____ b.   She coached the U.S. team in the Olympics.

_____ c.   Stanford offered her a coaching job.

_____ d.   Her friends and family thought moving was a bad idea.

_____ e.   She coached her 800th winning game.

_____ f.   She was a successful coach at Ohio State University.

B. Answer the questions. Write complete sentences.

1. When did Stanford offer VanDerveer the job?

_____

2. Why did VanDerveer accept the job?

_____

3. Why did her friends and family think she made a bad decision?

_____

4. When did she take a break from college coaching?

_____

5. What medal did her team win at the Olympics?

_____

WHAT DO YOU THINK?

A. Complete the activities. Then discuss your answers with a partner.

1. Read these phrases about Tara VanDeveer. For each phrase, write *D* for decision or *E* for event. A decision is a choice. An event is something that happens.

   a. _E_ 1996 Summer Olympics

   b. ___ took a break in 1995

   c. ___ accepted job at Stanford

   d. ___ team won four championships

   e. ___ team won the gold medal

   f. ___ wrote a book

2. For VanDerveer, what was probably the most important event? What was the most important decision?

   _____

   _____

Tip **Critical Thinking**

In Activity B, you **compare** Wood and VanDeveer to people you know about. When you connect new information with information you already know, you will understand the ideas better.

B. Think about both Reading 1 and Reading 2. Answer the questions in your notebook. Then discuss them with a partner.

1. Can you think of a person like John Wood or Tara VanDerveer? How is the person similar to Wood or VanDeveer? What does/did this person do?

2. Are you more interested in John Wood or Tara VanDerveer? Why? Where can you find more information about this person?

John Wood

Tara VanDerveer

Most words have several meanings. When you use a dictionary, first find the word and the correct word form (noun, verb, adjective, etc.). Then scan the definitions. **Choose the correct definition** for the context of the word. (The *context* is the sentence the word is in.)

> Wood wanted to give something **valuable** to children—education.

Read the definitions. The correct definition for the context in the sentence above is definition 2.

---

val·u·a·ble 🔑 /ˈvælyəbl/ *adjective*
1 worth a lot of money: *Is this ring valuable?*
2 very useful: *The book contains some valuable information.*

All dictionary entries are from the *Oxford Basic American Dictionary for learners of English* © Oxford University Press 2011.

A. Read the sentences on page 159. Then scan the definitions below. Write the correct definition number next to each sentence.

---

con·tin·ue 🔑 /kənˈtɪnyu/ *verb* (con·tin·ues, con·tin·u·ing, con·tin·ued)
1 to not stop happening or doing something: *If the pain continues, see your doctor.* • *The rain continued all afternoon.*
2 to start again after stopping: *Let's have lunch now and continue the meeting this afternoon.*
3 to go farther in the same direction: *We continued along the path until we came to the river.*

---

or·gan·i·za·tion 🔑 /ˌɔrɡənəˈzeɪʃn/ *noun*
1 [*count*] a group of people who work together for a special purpose: *He works for an organization that helps old people.*
2 [*noncount*] the activity of planning or arranging something; the way that something is planned or arranged: *She's busy with the organization of her daughter's wedding.*

---

dream¹ 🔑 /drim/ *noun* [*count*]
1 pictures or events that happen in your mind when you are asleep: *I had a **dream about** school last night.* ⊃ Look at **nightmare**.
2 something nice that you hope for: *His dream was to give up his job and live in the country.*

---

poor 🔑 /pʊr/ *adjective* (poor·er, poor·est)
1 with very little money: *She was too poor to buy clothes for her children.* • *She gave her life to helping **the poor** (= poor people).* ⊃ The noun is **poverty**. ⊃ ANTONYM **rich**
2 a word that you use when you feel sad because someone has problems: *Poor Tina! She's not feeling well.*
3 bad: *My grandfather is in very poor health.*

___ a.   Wood's **dream** was to bring books and education to children around the world.

___ b.   In 2000, he started an **organization**, Room to Read.

___ c.   Stanford University had a very **poor** basketball team.

___ d.   VanDeveer **continues** to coach, bringing top high school players to the university.

Tip for Success

Some words have the same word form for the noun and the verb. For example: *I had a* **dream** *about school last night. I often* **dream** *about school.*

B. Complete each sentence with one of the words from Activity A. Write the correct definition number next to each sentence.

_2_ a.   The school concert was terrific. The ___organization___ of the event was excellent.

___ b.   My grandfather's family was very _____. They didn't have much money.

___ c.   The boy woke up in the middle of the night. He had a bad _____.

___ d.   After you turn on First Street, _____ straight ahead to the traffic light.

___ e.   Anna is a _____ student. She's lazy and she doesn't study.

___ f.   My _____ did not seem possible, but I finally won a school race.

___ g.   Let's take break for lunch. We can _____ studying for the test after lunch.

___ h.   This _____ helps residents improve their neighborhood.

neighborhood improvements

WRITING

The simple past describes completed actions in the past.

> Last summer, he **decided** to attend a community college.
> I **graduated** from high school last year.

Many verbs have irregular past forms. (They don't end in *-ed*.) For a list, see page 166.

Irregular past forms

come	**came**	give	**gave**	leave	**left**	spend	**spent**
do	**did**	go	**went**	make	**made**	take	**took**
get	**got**	have	**had**	see	**saw**	write	**wrote**

Affirmative statements

subject	verb	
I - You - We - They	**moved**	to this city in 2009.
He - She - It	**came**	to my house last night.

- For affirmative statements, use the same past form for all subjects.

Negative statements

subject	*did + not*	verb	
I - You - We - They	**did not**	**continue**	the game.
He - She - It	**didn't**	**come**	to class yesterday.

- For negative statements, use *did not* + the base verb for both regular and irregular verbs.

Yes/No questions				Short answers	
did	subject	verb		*yes*	*no*
Did	they	**move**	to Miami?	Yes, they **did.**	No, they **didn't.**
Did	she	**come**	here?	Yes, she **did.**	No, she **didn't.**

Information questions				Answers
wh- word	*be*	subject	verb	past verb
Who		you	**see?**	I **saw** the coach.
What	**did**	the coach	**say?**	She **said**, "No."
Where		the players	**go?**	They **went** to the gym.

A. Complete the sentences. Use the correct form of the irregular verb. Some sentences need the negative form.

1. I ____didn't meet____ (not, meet) my friends today. I met them last night.

2. Last night Mika _____ (give) her friend some advice about college.

3. Mika _____ (tell) her friend about her college classes.

4. Sarah's family _____ (come) to this country five years ago.

5. My team _____ (win) the championship last year. We were very excited.

6. We _____ (not, leave) at 10:30. We left at noon.

7. Last year, Emma _____ (have) trouble with her math class.

8. David _____ (not, speak) English when he came here. He spoke Spanish.

9. I _____ (send) you an email last night.

10. Yesterday Sam _____ (take) a driving test. Fortunately, he passed it.

a driving test

B. Complete the questions with *you* and the correct form of the verb. Then answer the questions. Use complete sentences.

1. Where _____ *did you go* _____ (go) yesterday?

   I went to school, and in the afternoon I went to soccer practice.

2. _____ (take) a test last week?

   _____

3. Who _____ (speak) with last night?

_____

4. _____ (have) lunch at school yesterday?

_____

5. Who _____ (send) an email to yesterday?

_____

6. How _____ (get) to school today?

_____

7. How much money _____ (spend) yesterday?

_____

8. Who _____ (see) last weekend?

_____

Writing Skill | Showing sequence

1. Use **sequence words**—*first, next, after that, then,* and *finally*—to show the order of events. Use a comma after a sequence word. The words *next, then,* and *after that* have the same meaning. You can use them in any order.

> **First**, he listened to his coach.
> **Next**, he practiced with his team.
> **Then**, he spoke with his teammates.
> **After that**, he collected the sports equipment.
> **Finally**, he left the baseball field and went home.

2. **Past time expressions** help us to understand sequence. Past time expressions can come at the beginning or the end of a sentence. You usually use a comma when time expressions come at the beginning of a sentence.

> They went to Venezuela **last year**.   **Last year**, they went to Venezuela.
> He left **three hours ago**.   **Three hours ago**, he left.
> He joined the organization **in 2010**.   **In 2010**, he joined the organization.

for Success

The sequence expression "after that" means "after that time." You can use *after* + a time expression or an event. For example: *after 2009, after dinner, after graduation.*

A. Complete the paragraph. Use time expressions and sequence words from the box. Use capital letters at the beginning of sentences.

after college	after high school	finally	first
in 1953	in 1985	next	

    Tara VanDerveer was born _____ in Boston, Massachusetts. _____, she attended Indiana State University. She majored in sociology and she was a top basketball player. _____, she had several jobs. _____, she coached basketball at Idaho State University. _____, she moved to Ohio State in 1980. _____, she went to Stanford University _____. Her decision to go to Stanford University changed her life because she created an extraordinary team. Today she feels very good about her decision.

B. In your notebook, write a paragraph about yesterday. Use and underline time expressions and sequence words. Answer some of these questions.

What time did you get up?
What did you do after you got up?
What did you do after breakfast?
What did you do in the morning?

When did you have lunch?
What did you do after lunch?
What did you do in the evening?
Who did you talk with in the evening?

> Yesterday was a busy day. First, I got up at 6:00. I took a shower and washed my hair. After that, I got dressed. Next, I had toast and coffee for breakfast. After breakfast, I . . .

In this assignment, you write a paragraph about an event in your life. Think about the Unit Question, "What events change our lives?" and use the Self-Assessment checklist on page 165.

A. **BRAINSTORM** Follow these steps.

1. In your notebook, make a time line of some events in your life.

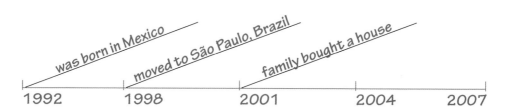

was born in Mexico / moved to São Paulo, Brazil / family bought a house

1992   1998   2001   2004   2007

2. Circle two important events in your time line.

3. Explain your time line to a partner. Discuss the two important events.

B. **WRITE** Choose one or two events in your life. Answer these questions. (You do not have to write complete sentences.) Then write a paragraph about the event(s) in your notebook. Use past time expressions and sequence words.

1. When did it happen? _____

2. Where did it happen? _____

3. Who was there? _____

4. What happened? _____

_____

_____

5. How did you feel? _____

_____

6. Why was it an important event? _____

_____

C. **REVISE** Read your partner's paragraph. Write two questions about the paragraph. Read and answer your partner's questions. Then revise and rewrite your paragraph.

D. EDIT Review your paragraph and complete the Self-Assessment checklist. Make any final changes. Be prepared to hand in your work or discuss it in class.

SELF-ASSESSMENT		
Yes	No	
☐	☐	Does every sentence have a subject and a verb?
☐	☐	Does the paragraph have correct format?
☐	☐	Check every verb. Is it the correct tense? Is it spelled correctly?
☐	☐	Do you use time expressions and sequence words?

Track Your Success

Circle the words you learned in this unit.

Nouns
career 🔑
championship
dream 🔑
opportunity 🔑
organization 🔑

Verbs
believe 🔑
continue 🔑
decide 🔑

promise 🔑
turn (something) into
   (something)

Adjectives
challenging AWL
poor 🔑
strong 🔑
successful 🔑
top 🔑
valuable 🔑

Adverb
even 🔑

Time and Sequence
after that
ago 🔑
finally 🔑 AWL
first 🔑
in (2010) 🔑
last (year) 🔑
next 🔑
then 🔑

🔑 Oxford 2000 keywords
AWL Academic Word List

Check (✓) the skills you learned. If you need more work on a skill, refer to the page(s) in parentheses.

READING ●	I can build reading fluency. (p. 151)
VOCABULARY ●	I can choose the correct definition from the dictionary. (p. 158)
GRAMMAR ●	I can use the simple past with regular and irregular verbs. (p. 160)
WRITING ●	I can use sequence words and time expressions to show sequence. (p. 162)
LEARNING OUTCOME ●	I can write a paragraph about an important event in my life. (p. 164)

COMMON IRREGULAR VERBS

Base form verb	Past form	Base form verb	Past form
be	was, were	know	knew
become	became	leave	left
begin	began	lose	lost
break	broke	make	made
bring	brought	meet	met
build	built	pay	paid
buy	bought	put	put
catch	caught	read	read
come	came	ride	rode
cut	cut	say	said
do	did	see	saw
drive	drove	send	sent
eat	ate	set	set
fight	fought	sit	sat
find	found	spend	spent
forget	forgot	stand	stood
get	got	take	took
give	gave	tell	told
go	went	think	thought
grow	grew	understand	understood
have	had	wear	wore
hear	heard	win	won
keep	kept	write	wrote